THE SONGS OF BILITIS

PIERRE LOUŸS

The Songs of Bilitis

TRANSLATED BY MITCHELL S. BUCK

With an Introduction by
George Ross Ridge
LOUISIANA STATE UNIVERSITY

Capricorn Books, New York

CONTENTS

➤➤➤ ⫷⫷⫷

II. ELEGIACS AT MYTILENE

8

THE TOMB OF BILITIS

Introduction

IN *The Songs of Bilitis* Pierre Louÿs perpetrated one of the most famous hoaxes in modern French literature. This slender volume of erotic prose poems was not, as purported, a strange and unbowdlerized translation from the Greek of a famous (or, as it were, an infamous) Lesbian poetess of Sapphic antiquity. For in the mundane order of archaeological fact there simply never existed a hauntingly lyrical courtesan by the name of Bilitis. Rather, she sprang, like Athena from the head of Zeus, fully armed and bellicose, from the uniquely potent brew of Louÿs's recondite classicism, febrile imagination, and decadent sensitivity. Bilitis was merely a phantom whom her doting creator had garbed with the seeming flesh of historical actuality, replete with sundry notes, observations, and appendices and with a cunningly fictionalized biography. Such, indeed, was the stuff of Louÿs's dreaming.

The Songs of Bilitis is a vivid dream. It achieves a remarkable verisimilitude through a compilation of detail and an intensity of documentation. Yet, in the bric-à-brac of such a vision, it seizes upon far more than the mere appearance of reality. It also affixes itself upon the very substance of life. Bilitis lives. She banquets, composes, and even whores, so to speak, with much pagan zest and complacency. She is not at all a pre-Christian marionette, peremptorily manipulated in wooden postures by the pervasive strings of an omniscient author and then paraded about with pompous artificiality in the mosaic pastiches of cadenced prose poems.

The obverse is true. Bilitis is first and always herself and ever also master of herself. She expresses herself through her own, properly voluntary, thought and action. She is "undetermined," so to speak. Hence she enjoys the creditability and acceptance given to a living person. She behaves as if Louÿs has merely sketched out the general design of her character and then stepped back in obvious astonishment. His wonder, too, is the supreme compliment. For an author should and must evince surprise if his creation is plausible, in truth, and gains the reader's total acceptance as a being of flesh and sinew, of motive and deed, funda-

mentally unknown and even unknowable. Such, indeed, is the proper
scope and function of good literary characterization. Such, too, is the
balanced measure of Bilitis. As a personage in a work of art, she is not
only well drawn; she is also, rather, indelibly etched. She is unforget-
table. In her own right, she lives. She continues to live for succeeding
generations of readers.

For several reasons *The Songs of Bilitis* enjoys a secure and not altogether minor niche in nineteenth-century French literature. First, it
represents a variation and indeed culmination of the genre of the prose
poem, so propitiously heralded in Romanticism by Aloysius Bertrand's
Gaspard de la Nuit and later perfected by a veritable host of luminaries
including Charles Baudelaire himself. Second, it personifies the very
essence of the Parnassianism from which it wells forth in spirit and
form, while at the same time it remains unique, apart, and, in a manner,
unclassified and even unclassifiable. Third, it is, after a fashion, morally
putrescent, corrupt, gamy—in a word, "decadent." It is in this sense that
the work caught the immediate fancy of the jaded audience of the *fin
de siècle*. Perhaps in this sense, too, it has continued to titillate the
prurient sensibility of the more pornographically inclined to the present
day. Such an observation is not necessarily damning in itself. For example, many an adolescent, impelled by the longings of a nascent puberty,
has stumbled upon great art in his youthful quest for erotica. The supreme test, of course, is whether this same person will continue to read
the work forty years later. In this way, as its publishing history amply
attests, *The Songs of Bilitis* weathers supremely well the test of time and
the vagaries of adolescent motivation. For this volume of prose poems is
not merely "decadent," as the world glibly bandies the term about. It
is "Decadent." It is, indeed, by critical consensus, a Decadent masterpiece.

So, finally, the question arises: What is Decadence? The resolution
tends to be complex and perhaps deals more often in questions than with
answers.

In its preoccupation with the fall of a society, Decadent literature is
naturally concerned, and even obsessed, with those forces which set into
climactic motion the holocaust of the *Götterdämmerung*. So it is that a
Joséphin Péladan laments piously the collapse of a healthful bourgeois
morality in his epic roman-fleuve, *Finis Latinorum*. So, too, a Paul

Verlaine, rent in a titanic struggle between flesh and the spirit, pens his ethereal verses on carnal pleasures, and peoples the centuries with the boulevardiers, dandies, and pederasts of the derelict Second Empire. So, too, a Joris-Karl Huysmans, the archetypal Decadent writer, his own transfigured protagonist in fiction, vaporizes perfume tableaux in hothouses, and blends heady cordials from a rare liqueur cabinet, and takes emetics so that, like a Roman emperor, he can again suffer the ecstasy of gorging himself at another banquet of vulvae and sperm balls. In short, Decadent literature is a mosaic series of the portraits and depictions of a gamy assortment of homo duplexes, megalopolitans, aesthetes, perverts, vampires, and femmes fatales, with the occasional intimation of a super-annuated roué leering over his absinthe.

Decadent literature, then, is the embodiment of a pessimistic, jaded, and blasé world view of spleen, ennui, and corruption. It is the total yawn of absolute *Weltschmerz*. Society is rotten because the men and women who people it and give it direction have decayed and *fallen away* beyond spiritual redemption and ethical recall. *Après la décadence le déluge,* so to say. There is no presentiment of another social order emerging beyond the horizon. Such is not the Decadent's concern. He is solely preoccupied with the beauty and tragic grandeur of the decline and fall. Hence he paints the Legend of Imperial Rome, or waxes eloquent over the Carthaginian Wars, or loses himself in the voluptuous annihilation of Byzantium, or, on the contemporary scene, drowns his spleen in the innumerable absinthes of the Second Empire, basking in the mellow if not rotted name of Napoleon, just before the flaming sunset of Sedan. Certainly the images of Decadent literature are uniformly melancholy, for they reflect the *Zeitgeist* of a moribund society and capture the essence of perpetual defeat in which there is even a masochistic pleasure in the servile contemplation of one's utter enslavement and abasement.

Within this context *The Songs of Bilitis* exercises a different quality of appeal. It is the fascination of healthfulness. In the work Louÿs does not portray with a perverted scholar's involuted exactitude the minutiae of a forgotten civilization on an island lost to oblivion and the vicissitudes of time and taste. He rather makes a spot of verdant earth blossom again with pastoral charm. In the book Louÿs does not merely excite the invert's imagination with luxuriant prose and snatches of lurid love-making. He simply tells the story of an uncomplicated and sensitive young girl, Bilitis, who, as a bisexual, and normal, can love adolescent girls as well as boys, and who, in time, ripens, matures, and ages in the natural order of things. Louÿs recounts her adventures with exquisite restraint and supreme taste in little tableaux of perception. They are pearls of insight, and they serve as veritable models for the prose poem. They are, moreover, not only the tale of a young poetess's love for man and woman, but also of her absorption in poetry and the creative process. They are, most importantly, spots of time in the eternal process when the poetess, Bilitis, relates herself to the elements of earth and water, of time and the seasons, of love and sadness, of life and death. These prose poems are her diary. As such, they are a brilliant and memorable one. Bilitis turns the pages, day by day, year by year, to record her encounter with life, and regards her little Grecian world with a tough tenderness and a fierce sensitivity. She shows herself to be at once Sappho and more than Sappho. One can at least know Bilitis, whereas Sappho will remain forever at a distance. And in knowing Bilitis, one can love her. It is small wonder, then, that, with its peculiar appeal, *The Songs of Bilitis,* and its enigmatic vision of a masculine courtesan, immediately caught the jaded eye of the French *fin de siècle,* swept its audience with the clean breath of pristine enthusiasm, and gained the renown as a Decadent masterpiece which it still enjoys today.

GEORGE ROSS RIDGE

Louisiana State University
Baton Rouge, Louisiana

THE SONGS OF BILITIS

＊≫≫≪≪＊

TRANSLATED BY

MITCHELL · S · BUCK

TRANSLATOR'S NOTE

≫≫≪≪

THE Songs of Bilitis, Pierre Louÿs' great sequence of prose poems on
an antique theme, was first published in 1894. The title-page of the
first edition was lettered, simply, "Translated from the Greek," and
this suggestion of translation was strengthened by the inclusion of a
"Bibliography" and by recording, in the Index, a number of Songs
marked "Not translated," which, as a matter of fact, never existed.
But it is extremely doubtful whether anyone acquainted with the Greek
Poets could have been misled into imagining that Bilitis—at least, as a
poetess—ever really existed. A number of passages indicate modern
thought: and some of the Songs, while not exactly translated, are
adapted from epigrams by well-known poets in the Greek Anthology.
"Philodemos," Pierre Louÿs remarks, however, "twice stole from her,"
as though to infer that Bilitis was the originator of these poems (CI
and CXXXII) attributed to Philodemos.

The greater number of the pastels and, of course, the conception
of the work as a whole, were entirely original with Pierre Louÿs; and
the resulting book is, perhaps, the most singular bloom of his genius, all
the more remarkable in that it was published in his twenty-third year.

Following an imaginary "Life of Bilitis," setting the key for the
Songs to follow, the book is divided into three parts. The first is a series
of delightful pastorals; the second narrates incidents of Bilitis' life on
the Isle of Lesbos; and the third her experiences while living as a courtesan on the Isle of Kypros.

In the Notes at the end of the present edition, such direct transla-
tions or paraphrases from antique writers as I have been able to identify,
have been indicated, with occasional comment, for the information of
the reader.

The work has been more or less known to cultured American
readers since the issue, in 1904, of the scholarly pioneer translation by
Dr. Horace Manchester Brown. My first translation, made about six-

teen years ago, and published in 1919, has been revised throughout for the present edition and the Notes have been augmented.

I have endeavored to retain, in the translation, the full sense of the original text and yet to give the English version a reasonable amount of that euphony which is so essential in works of this kind. Where unbroken rhythm in the translation would have required amplification or curtailment of literal precision, I have sacrificed rhythm as of secondary importance. In fact, the essential characteristic of successful prose poems, of the pattern used by Pierre Louÿs, is a simple directness, of the kind so noticeable in the Greek Epigram, coupled with a rounding out of the final sentences into a full period, completing both the thought and the acoustic effect. How Pierre Louÿs excelled in meeting these conditions is readily perceptible, even in translation.

MITCHELL S. BUCK

August, 1928

LIFE OF BILITIS

≫≫ ≪≪

BILITIS was born at the beginning of the sixth century before our era, in a mountain village situated on the banks of the Melas, towards the eastern part of Pamphylia. This country is stony and sad, shadowed by profound forests, dominated by the enormous mass of Tauros; lime springs issue from the rocks, great salty lakes abide on the heights, and the valleys are replete with silence.

She was the daughter of a Greek and of a Phœnician woman. She seems never to have known her father, for he has no part in any of the remembrances of her childhood. Perhaps he had died before she came into the world. Otherwise, it would be difficult to explain how she bore a Phœnician name which her mother alone could have given her.

In this almost deserted land, she lived a tranquil life with her mother and her sisters. Other young girls, who were her friends, lived not far from her. On the woody slopes of Tauros, the shepherds pastured their flocks.

In the morning, at cock-crow, she arose, went to the stable, led the animals to drink and busied herself milking them. During the day, if it rained, she remained in the gynæceum and spun the wool of her distaff. If the weather was fair, she ran in the fields and played, with her companions, many games of which she tells us.

Bilitis regarded the Nymphs with ardent piety. The sacrifices which she offered were nearly always for their fountain. She often speaks of them but it seems that she never saw them, for she reports with so much veneration the accounts of an old man who, one day, had surprised them.

The end of her pastoral existence was saddened by a love of which we know little, although she speaks of it at length. She ceased to sing of it when it became unhappy. Having become the mother of a child which she abandoned, Bilitis left Pamphylia for unknown reasons and never returned to the place of her birth.

We find her again at Mytilene, where she had come by way of the sea, along the fair coasts of Asia. She was then scarcely sixteen years old, according to the conjectures of M. Heim, who established with probability some dates in the life of Bilitis from a verse which alludes to the death of Pittakos.

Lesbos was then the centre of the world. On the main road be-

tween beautiful Attica and magnificent Lydia, it had for its capital a
city more elegant than Athens and more corrupt than Sardis: Mytilene,
built upon a peninsula overlooking the shores of Asia. The blue sea
encompassed the city. From the height of the temples, one could dis-
tinguish, on the horizon, the white line of Atarnea which was the port
of Pergamos.

The narrow streets were always encumbered by a throng re-
splendent in many-colored stuffs: tunics of purple and of hyacinth,
cyclas of transparent silks, mantles trailing in the dust of the yellow
shoes. The women bore in their ears great rings of gold set with raw
pearls, and on their arms massive bracelets of silver roughly chiseled in
relief. The men themselves wore their hair shining and perfumed with
rare oils. The ankles of the Greeks were bare in the fastenings of their
sandals, wide bands of bright metal which tinkled at their heels; those
of the Asiatics were covered by soft, tinted boots. The passers-by stood
in groups before the façades of the shops, where all the goods for sale
were on display: rugs of sombre colors, cloths worked with threads of
gold, jewels of amber and of ivory, according to the quarter. The
animation of Mytilene did not end with the day; there was no hour so
late that one could not hear, through the open doors, the joyous sounds
of instruments, the cries of women and the noise of dances. Pittakos
himself, who wished to give a little order to this perpetual debauch,
made a law in defense of flute players too young to be employed in the
nocturnal festivals; but this law, like all laws which endeavor to change
the course of natural morals, determined the secrecy but not the
observance.

In a society where husbands were occupied at night with wine and
dancing-girls, the women could not fail to unite and find, among
themselves, consolation for their solitude. Thus it was that they softened
to those delicate loves to which antiquity has given their name and
which have, whatever men may think, more of true passion than of
studied viciousness.

At this time, Sappho was still beautiful. Bilitis knew her and
speaks of her under the name of Psappha [1] which she bore at Lesbos.
Without doubt, she was the admirable woman who taught the little
Pamphylian the art of singing in rhythmic phrases and of conserving
for posterity the remembrance of her loves. Unfortunately, Bilitis has
given us few details of this woman, today so little known; and this is
to be regretted, since the least word is precious which touches that great
Inspiration. Instead, she has left us, in thirty elegies, the history of her
love for a young girl of her own age whom she calls Mnasidika and
who lived with her. We already knew the name of this young girl

from a verse of Sappho's [2] in which her beauty is exalted; but even the name is doubtful, and Bergk is inclined to think that she called herself simply Mnais. The Songs we shall read later on prove that this hypothesis may be abandoned. Mnasidika seems to have been a little girl, very sweet and very innocent, one of those charming persons whose mission is to permit themselves to be adored, so much the more cherished since they make few efforts to merit that which is given them. Loves without motives last the longest; this one endured for ten years. One knows how it was broken through the fault of Bilitis whose excessive jealousy understood no eclecticism.

When she felt that nothing held her longer at Mytilene except unhappy memories, Bilitis made a second voyage; she went to Kypros, an island Greek and Phœnician like Pamphylia itself, which must have recalled to her memory the aspect of her native country.

It was there that Bilitis began her life for the third time and in a manner my readers will understand with difficulty unless they recall the point to which love was considered holy among the peoples of antiquity. The courtesans of Amathus were not, like ours, lost creatures, exiled from all worldly society; they were girls from the best families of the city. Aphrodite had given them beauty and they thanked the goddess by consecrating to the service of her worship the beauty they had received. All the cities, like those of Kypros, which possessed a temple rich in courtesans, regarded those women with careful respect.

The incomparable history of Phryne,[3] as transmitted to us by Athenæus, gives some idea of the nature of this veneration. It is not true that it was necessary for Hyperides to strip her naked in order to soften the Areopagos, although her crime was great: she had committed murder. The orator tore off the top of her tunic and revealed only her breasts. And he supplicated the judges: "Do not put to death the priestess and the inspired of Aphrodite."

In distinction from the other courtesans, who went out in transparent cyclas through which all the details of their bodies were visible, Phryne was accustomed to envelop herself, even to her hair, in one of those great, folded vestments of which the statuettes of Tanagra have preserved the grace. No one, unless it were her lovers, had ever seen her arms or her shoulders, and she never appeared in the pool of the public baths. But one day an extraordinary thing occurred. It was the day of the festival of Eleusis; twenty thousand people, from all parts of Greece, had assembled on the seashore when Phryne advanced to the waves. She removed her garment, she unfastened her cincture, she removed even her under-tunic. "She unrolled her hair and she entered into the sea." And in that throng stood Praxiteles who, after this living

goddess, designed the Aphrodite of Knidos; and Apelles who glimpsed
the form of his Anadyomene. Admirable people, to whom naked Beauty
could appear without exciting laughter or false shame!

I wish that this history were that of Bilitis for, in translating her
Songs, I have learned to love the friend of Mnasidika. Without doubt,
her life also was wonderful. I regret only that she is not spoken of
oftener and that the ancient authors, at least those whose works have
survived, give us so little information about her. Philodemos, who twice
stole from her, does not even mention her name. In default of better
anecdotes, I beg that you will be contented with the details which she
herself has given us about her life as a courtesan. That she was a courtesan is undeniable; and even her last Songs prove that, if she had the
virtues of her vocation, she had also its worst weaknesses. But I would
know only her virtues. She was pious and skilful. She remained faithful
to the temple so long as Aphrodite consented to prolong the youth of
her purest devotee. The day when she ceased to be loved, she ceased to
write, she said. Nevertheless, it is difficult to admit that the Songs of
Pamphylia could have been written at the epoch when the events took
place. How could a little shepherdess of the mountains learn to scan
verses according to the difficult rhythms of the Æolic tradition? It is
more reasonable to believe that, having become old, Bilitis found
pleasure in singing for herself the memories of her distant childhood.
We know nothing about this last period of her life. We know not even
at what age she died.

Her tomb was found by M. G. Heim, at Paleo-Limisso, at the side
of an antique road, not far from the ruins of Amathus. These ruins
have almost disappeared during the last thirty years and the stones of
the house where perhaps Bilitis lived, today pave the quays of Port Said.
But the tomb was subterranean, according to the Phœnician custom, and
it had escaped even the treasure-hunters.

M. Heim entered it through a narrow well, filled with earth, at the
bottom of which he found a walled-up door which had to be demol-
ished. The wide, low tomb, paved with slabs of limestone, had four
walls covered with plaques of black amphibolite, on which were graven,
in primitive capitals, all the Songs we are about to read, except the three
Epitaphs, which decorated the sarcophagus.

There reposed the friend of Mnasidika, in a large coffin of terra-
cotta, under a cover modeled in delicate sculpture which figured in clay
the visage of the dead. The hair was painted black, the eyes were half
closed and prolonged by the crayon as though she were living, and the
painted cheek was softened by a slight smile which brought out the lines
of the mouth. Nothing can describe the lips, at once delicate and slightly

curling, soft and pure, united one to the other and as though intoxicated by their own union.

When the coffin was opened, she appeared in the state in which a pious hand had placed her, twenty-four centuries before. Vials of perfume hung from pegs of clay, and one of these, after so long a time, was still fragrant. The mirror of polished silver in which Bilitis had viewed herself, the stylus which had trailed the blue pigment over her eyelids, were found in their place. A little naked Astarte, relic forever precious, watched always over the skeleton ornamented with all its jewels of gold and white like a snowy branch, but so soft and so fragile that, at the first breath of air, it crumbled, and mingled with the dust.

PIERRE LOUŸS

Constantinople, August, 1894

I
BUCOLICS IN PAMPHYLIA

I. BUCOLICS IN PAMPHYLIA

'Αδύ δέ μοι τὸ μέλισμα, καὶ ἤν σύριγγι μελίσδω
κῆν αὐλῷ λάλεω, κῆν δώνακι,
κῆν πλαγιαύλῳ.

THEOCRITOS[4]

>>> <<<

I

THE TREE

STRIPPED of my clothes, I climbed into a tree; my bare thighs embraced the smooth, moist bark; my sandals trod upon the branches.

Far up, yet under the leaves and shadowed from the heat, I placed myself astride a projecting branch and balanced my feet in the void.

It had rained. The water drops fell and slipped over my skin. My hands were stained with moss and my toes were reddened from crushed flowers.

When the wind passed, I felt the life of the beautiful tree. Then I pressed my legs yet closer and laid my open lips upon the hairy nape of a bough.

II

PASTORAL SONG

LET us sing a pastoral song, invoking Pan, god of the wind of summer. Selenis and I each watch our flocks, from the round shadow of an olive tree which trembles.

Selenis lies upon the meadow. She raises herself and runs, or searches for grasshoppers, or gathers flowers and herbs, or bathes her face in the cool water of the brook.

And I—I draw the wool from the white backs of the sheep to garnish my distaff, and I spin. The hours move slowly. In the sky, an eagle passes.

The shadow turns; let us move the basket of flowers and the jar of milk. Let us sing a pastoral song, invoking Pan, god of the wind of summer.

III

MATERNAL ADVICE

M Y mother bathes me in the shadow, she dresses me in the bright sunlight and binds my hair in the light of lamps; but if I walk out in the moonlight, she draws my girdle into a double knot.

She says to me: "Play with virgins, dance with little children; look not out of the window, shun the words of young men and turn from the counsel of widows.

"Some evening, someone will come to carry thee, like the others, over the threshold, amidst a great assemblage of sonorous drums and amorous flutes.

"That evening, when thou goest away, Bilito, thou wilt leave me three gourds of gall: one for the morning, one for midday and the third, the bitterest, the third for the days of festival."

IV

THE NAKED FEET

I H A V E black hair all the length of my back and a small round cap. My chiton is of white wool. My legs are fast browned by the sun.

If I lived in the city, I should wear jewels of gold and gilded chitons and shoes of silver.... I regard my naked feet in their slippers of dust.

Psophis! Come here, little beggar! Carry me to the spring, bathe my feet in thy hands and press olives and violets to perfume them like flowers.

Today thou shalt be my slave, thou shalt follow me and serve me; and, at the end of the day, I will give thee, for thy mother, lentils from the garden of mine.

V

THE OLD MAN AND THE NYMPHS

A B L I N D old man lives upon the mountain. For having looked upon the nymphs, his eyes died, long ago. And, since, his happiness is a distant memory.

"Yes, I have seen them," he said to me. "Helopsychria, Limnanthis: they were standing near the bank, in the green pool of Physos. The water sparkled higher than their knees.

"Their necks inclined beneath their long hair. Their nails were thin as the wings of grasshoppers. Their nipples were hollowed like the cups of hyacinths.

"They trailed their fingers upon the water and drew up, from an invisible vase, the long-stemmed water-lilies. Around their parted thighs, the ripples slowly widened."

VI
SONG

"TORI-TORTUE, what doest thou among us?—I wind the wool and the thread of Milet.—Alas! Alas! Why dost thou not dance?—I am too sorrowful. I am too sorrowful.

"Tori-tortue, what doest thou among us?—I cut a reed for a funereal flute.—Alas! Alas! What has befallen him?—I will not tell. I will not tell.

"Tori-tortue, what doest thou among us?—I press the olives for oil for the stele.—Alas! Alas! And who, then, is dead?—Canst thou ask? Canst thou ask?

"Tori-tortue, what doest thou among us?—He has fallen into the sea . . .—Alas! Alas! And how was that?—From the backs of white horses. From the backs of white horses."

VII
THE PASSER-BY

As I was seated in the evening before the door of the house, a young man passed by. He looked at me; I turned aside my head. He spoke to me but I did not answer.

He wished to approach me. I took a sickle from the wall and I would have cut open his cheek if he had advanced a step.

Then, drawing back a little, he began to smile and he breathed in his hand toward me, saying: "Receive a kiss." And I cried! And I wept! So much so that my mother ran to me,

Alarmed, fearing I had been stung by a scorpion. I wept: "He kissed me!" My mother also kissed me and carried me away in her arms.

VIII
THE AWAKENING

It is already daylight. I should be up. But the drowsiness of morning is sweet and the warmth of my bed enfolds me closer. I long to remain abed.

Soon I shall go to the stable. I shall give the goats grass and flowers and a flask of fresh water drawn from the well where I shall drink with them.

Then I shall fasten them to the post and milk their soft, warm udders; and, if the kids are not too jealous, I will suck with them from the supple teats.

Amaltheia: did she not feed Zeus? Then I will go. But not yet. The sun has risen too soon and my mother is not yet awake.

IX

THE RAIN

THE fine rain has wet everything, very gently and in silence. It still rains a little. I will go out among the trees—my feet naked, so I shall not stain my shoes.

The rain of springtime is delicious. The branches, laden with moist flowers, have a perfume which bewilders me. The sun sparkles on the delicate bark.

Alas! How many flowers upon the ground! How pitiful, these flowers which have fallen. They should not be swept aside and mingled with the mud, but saved for the bees.

The beetles and snails traverse the path between the puddles of water. I will not tread upon them nor frighten the golden lizard who stretches out, blinking his eyelids.

X

THE FLOWERS

NYMPHS of the woods and fountains, sweetest of friends, I am here. Do not hide yourselves, but come to my aid, for I am laden with many flowers.

I wish to choose, from all the forest, a poor hamadryad with raised arms, and in her hair, the color of leaves, I shall place my largest rose.

See: I have taken so many from the fields that I cannot carry them away unless you help me to make a garland. If you refuse, beware:

She of you with the orange hair, I saw her yesterday embraced like a beast by the satyr Lamprosathes and I will denounce the shameless one.

XI
IMPATIENCE

I THREW myself into her arms and wept, and, for a long time, she felt my hot tears roll over her shoulder, before my sorrow would let me speak:

"Alas! I am only a child; the young men never look at me. When shall I have, like thee, a young woman's breasts to raise my robe and entice kisses?

"There are no curious eyes if my tunic slips; no one gathers up the flower which falls from my hair, nor does anyone threaten to kill me if my mouth is given to another."

She replied to me, tenderly: "Bilitis, little virgin, thou criest like a cat at the moon and thou art troubled without reason. The girls who are the most impatient are not the soonest chosen."

XII
COMPARISONS

SPARROW,[5] bird of Kypris, sing with our first desires! The fresh bodies of young girls bloom with flowers like the earth. The night of all our dreams approaches and we talk of it among ourselves.

Sometimes we compare, all together, the differences in our beauties, our hair already long, our young breasts still small, our puberties like little round quails hiding under the nascent down.

Yesterday I competed thus with Melantho, who is older than I. She was proud of her breasts which had grown in a month and, pointing to my straight tunic, she called me "Little Child."

No man could see us; we compared ourselves naked before the girls: and, if she vanquished me on one point, I far surpassed her on all others. Sparrow, bird of Kypris, sing with our first desires!

XIII
THE FOREST RIVER

I BATHED myself, alone, in the forest river. I am sure I frightened the naiads, for I divined them moving anxiously in the depths of the dark water.

I called them. To resemble them better, I plaited upon my neck irises black as my hair and clusters of yellow gilliflowers.

From a long, floating herb, I made myself a green girdle and, to see it, I pressed up my breasts and inclined my head a little.

And I called: "Naiads! Naiads! Play with me; be kind." But the naiads are transparent and perhaps, without knowing, I have caressed their delicate arms.

XIV
COME, MELISSA

W H E N the sun becomes less burning, we will go and play upon the river banks, we will struggle for a frail crocus or for a damp hyacinth.

We will form a round ring and weave a garland; we will take each other by the hand and by the ends of our tunics.

Come, Melissa![6] Give us honey. Come, Naiads! We will bathe with you. Come, Melissa! Throw a gentle shadow over our perspiring bodies.

And we will offer you, kind Nymphs, not shameful wine, but oil and milk and goats with twisted horns.

XV
THE SYMBOLIC RING

V O Y A G E R S who return from Sardis tell us that the women of Lydia are covered with collars and stones from the top of their hair to their tinted feet.

The girls of my country have neither bracelets nor diadems, but one of their fingers carries a silver ring and upon the bezel is graven the triangle of the Goddess.

When they turn the point outward, they mean: "Psyche is to be taken." When they turn the point inward, they mean: "Psyche is taken."

The men believe this; the women do not. As for me, I care little which way the point is turned, for Psyche offers herself freely. Psyche is always to be taken.

XVI
DANCES BY MOONLIGHT

O N the soft grass, in the night, the young girls with hair of violets have danced together, one of each pair answering for the lover.

The virgins said: "We are not for you." And, as though they

were bashful, they hid their virginity. Among the trees, an ægipan
played upon the flute.

The others said: "You will come to seek us." They had gathered
in their robes like the tunics of men, and they struggled gently, entwin-
ing their dancing legs.

Then each, acknowledging herself as vanquished, took her friend
by the ears, like a cup with two handles,[7] and, including the head, drank
a kiss.

XVII

THE LITTLE CHILDREN

THE river is almost dry; the brittle reeds are dying in the mud; the
air burns and, far beyond the hollowed banks, a clear brook flows
over the gravel.

It is there that, from morning to evening, the little naked children
come to play. They bathe themselves, but no higher than their calves,
for the river is low.

But they walk in the current, sometimes slipping on the rocks;
and the little boys throw water on the little girls, who laugh.

And, when a troop of passing merchants lead their great white
oxen to drink, they clasp their hands behind them and watch the enormous beasts.

XVIII

THE STORIES

I AM loved by the little children; when they see me, they run to me
and cling to my tunic or clasp my legs in their little arms.

If they have gathered flowers, they give them all to me; if they
have caught a beetle, they put it in my hand; if they have nothing,
they caress me and make me sit before them.

Then they kiss me on the cheek, they rest their heads upon my
breasts; they supplicate me with their eyes. I know well what they
wish to say.

They wish to say: "Dear Bilitis, tell us, for we are quiet, the
history of Perseus the hero, or of the death of little Hellé."[8]

XIX

THE MARRIED FRIEND

OUR mothers were pregnant at the same time and, this evening, she
is married, Melissa, my dearest friend. The roses are still upon the
path; the torches have not yet burned out.

And I return, by the same path, with my mother; and I dream. Thus, what she is today, I could be also. Am I not already a grown girl?

The cortège, the flutes, the nuptial song and the flowered car of the bridegroom, all the festival, some other evening, will unfold for me under the branches of the olives.

 • Like Melissa at this same hour, I shall unveil myself before a man, I shall know love in the night; and, later, little children shall nourish themselves at my swollen breasts. . . .

XX
CONFIDENCES

T H E next day, I went to her house, and we blushed when we saw each other. She led me into her chamber where we could be alone.

I had many things to say to her, but when I saw her I forgot them all. I did not even dare throw myself upon her neck; I regarded her high girdle.

I was astonished that nothing in her face had changed, that she still resembled my friend although, since the sleepless night, she had learned so many things which frightened me.

Suddenly, I seated myself upon her knees, took her in my arms, and whispered quickly, anxiously, into her ear. Then she laid her cheek against mine and told me all.

XXI
THE MOON WITH EYES OF BLUE

N I G H T mingles with the hair of women and the branches of the willows. I walked at the edge of the water. Suddenly I heard singing; then only I knew that young girls were there.

I said to them: "Of whom do you sing?" They replied: "Of those who return." One awaited her father, another her brother; but she who awaited her lover was the most impatient.

They had woven for themselves crowns and garlands cut from the branches of palms and lotos drawn from the water. They rested their arms on each others' necks and sang, one after another.

I moved along the river, saddened and all alone; but, looking about me, I saw, behind the great trees, the moon with eyes of blue conducting me.

XXII
SONG

"Shadow of the woods, whence she should come: tell me, where has my mistress gone?—She has descended upon the plain.—Plain, where has my mistress gone?—She has followed the banks of the river."

"Fair river, who hast seen her pass, tell me: is she near this place? —She has left me for the path.—Path, dost thou see her still?—She has left me for the road."

"O white road, road of the city, tell me: where hast thou led her?—To the street of gold which enters into Sardis.—O street of light, touchest thou her naked feet?—She has entered the palace of the king."

"O palace, splendor of the earth, return her to me.—See! She has collars on her breasts and circlets in her hair, an hundred pearls along her legs, two arms around her waist."

XXIII
LYKAS

Come, we will go into the fields, under the thicket of juniper; we will eat honey from the hives, we will make snares for grasshoppers with the twigs of asphodels.

Come, we shall see Lykas, who tends his father's flocks on the slopes of shadowy Tauros. Surely he will give us milk.

Already I hear the sound of his flute. He plays most skilfully. Here are the dogs and the sheep and he himself standing against a tree. Is he not handsome as Adonis?

O Lykas! give us milk. Here are figs from our fig trees. We are going to rest with thee. Bearded goats, do not leap, for fear of exciting the restless bucks.

XXIV
THE OFFERING TO THE GODDESS

It is not for Artemis whom they adore at Perga, this garland woven by my hands, although Artemis may be a good goddess who will watch over my couches of pain.

It is not for Athena whom they adore at Sidon, although she

may be of ivory and of gold and carry in her hand a pomegranate which tempts the birds.

No, it is for Aphrodite, whom I adore in my heart, for she only can give me what my lips most need, if I hang on her sacred tree my garland of tender roses.

But I will not ask aloud that which I beg of her. I will raise myself upon my toes and confide my secret to a cleft in the bark.

XXV
THE COMPLAISANT FRIEND

THE storm continued all the night. Selenis of the beautiful hair had come to spin with me. She remained for fear of the mud and, pressed one against the other, we filled my little bed.

When girls lie together, sleep remains at the door. "Bilitis, tell me, tell me, whom lovest thou?" She slipped her leg over mine to caress me gently.

And she said, against my mouth: "I know, Bilitis, whom thou lovest. Close thine eyes. I am Lykas." I replied, touching her: "Do I not know thou art a girl? Thy jest fits badly."

But she replied: "In truth, I am Lykas if thou wilt close thine eyes. These are his arms, these are his hands. . . ." And tenderly, in the silence, she enchanted my reverie into a singular illusion.

XXVI
A PRAYER TO PERSEPHONE

PURIFIED by the ritual ablutions and clad in violet tunics, we have kissed toward the earth our hands laden with branches of olive.

"O Persephone of the Underworld, or whatever may be the name thou desirest: if this name is acceptable to thee, hear us, O Shadowy-Haired Queen, sterile and unsmiling.

"Kokhlis, daughter of Thrasymakos, is ill, and dangerously. Do not call her yet. Thou knowest she cannot escape thee; some day, much later, thou shalt take her.

"But drag her not away so soon, O Unseen Ruler! For she weeps because of her virginity; she supplicates thee through our prayers; and we will give, for her deliverance, three black unshorn ewes."

XXVII
THE GAME OF DICE

As we both loved him, we played for him with dice. It was a great match. Many young girls looked on.

She threw at first the cast of Kyklopes and I the cast of Solon. But she the Kallibolos and I, feeling myself lost, I prayed to the Goddess.

I played; I had the Epiphenon, she the terrible cast of Kios, I the Antiteukos, she the Trikias, and I the cast of Aphrodite which won the disputed lover.

But, seeing her pale, I threw my arm about her neck and said, close to her ear (so that she alone heard me): "Do not weep, little friend; we will let him choose between us."

XXVIII
THE DISTAFF

All the day, my mother has kept me in the gynæceum with my sisters whom I do not love and who talk among themselves in low voices. I, in a little corner, I spin my distaff.

Distaff, since I am alone with thee, it is to thee I will talk. With thy wig of white wool, thou art like an old woman. Listen to me.

If I could go, I would not be here, seated in the shadow of the wall and spinning wearily. I would be sleeping with the violets upon the slopes of Tauros.

Because he is so much poorer than I, my mother will not espouse me. However, I say to thee: either I will have no wedding day or it is he who shall carry me over the threshold.

XXIX
THE FLUTE

For the day of Hyacinthus, he gives me a syrinx made of carefully cut reeds united with white wax which is sweet as honey to my lips.

He teaches me to play, seated upon his knees; but I tremble a little. He plays after me, so softly that I can scarcely hear him.

We have nothing to say to each other, so near we are, one to the other; but our songs reply to each other and, by turns, our lips touch the reeds.

It is late; there is the song of the green frogs which begins with the night. My mother will never believe that I have stayed so long searching for my lost girdle.

XXX
THE HAIR

H E said to me: "Last night, I dreamed. I had thy hair about my neck. I had thy locks like a black collar about my neck and over my breast.

"I caressed them, and they were mine; and we were bound thus forever, by the same locks, mouth upon mouth, like two laurels with but a single root.

"And, little by little, it seemed to me that our limbs were mingled; that I became thyself and that thou didst enter into me like my dream."

When he had finished, he softly laid his hands upon my shoulders and looked at me with so tender a regard that I lowered my eyes, shivering.

XXXI
THE CUP

L Y K A S saw me coming, clad only in a little chiton, for the days were overwhelming. He wished to mould my breast, which was uncovered.

He took fine clay, kneaded in the fresh, clear water. When he laid it upon my skin, I thought I should faint, for the earth was very cold.

From my moulded breast, he made a cup, round and umbilicate. He placed it in the sun to dry and tinted it all over with the purple and ochre of crushed flowers.

Then we went to the fountain which is consecrated to the nymphs and threw the cup into the current, with stalks of gilliflowers.

XXXII
ROSES IN THE NIGHT

W H E N the night mounts into the sky, the world belongs to us and to the gods. We go over the fields to the spring, through the dark wood to the glades, wherever our naked feet lead us.

The little stars shine enough for such little shadows as we are. Sometimes, under the low branches, we find sleeping hinds.

But, more charming than all else in the night, is a place known only to ourselves, which attracts us through the forest: a thicket of mysterious roses.

For nothing in the world is so divine as the perfume of roses in the night. How is it that, in the time when I was alone, I never felt their ecstasy?

XXXIII
REMORSE

A T first I did not reply; shame flushed my cheeks and the beating of my heart distressed my breasts.

Then I resisted; I said: "No. No." I turned away my head and the kiss did not open my lips nor love my fast-closed knees.

Then he begged my forgiveness, he kissed my hair, I felt his burning breath, and he departed.... Now I am alone.

I regard the empty place, the deserted wood, the trampled earth. And I bite my fingers until they bleed and I smother my cries in the grass.

XXXIV
THE INTERRUPTED SLEEP

A L L alone I fell asleep, like a partridge in the heather.... The light wind, the sound of the waters, the sweetness of the night, all held me there.

Imprudently I slept and awakened with a cry; and I struggled, and I wept. But already it was too late. Of what use are the hands of a child?

He would not leave me. Rather, with greater tenderness, he drew me closer in his arms, and I saw in all the world neither the earth nor the trees but only the light in his eyes....

To thee, Kypris Victorious, I consecrate these offerings still moist with the dew, vestiges of the pains of virginity, witnesses of my sleep and of my resistance.

XXXV
THE WASH-WOMEN

W A S H - W O M E N , say not that you have seen me! I confide in you; do not repeat it! Between my tunic and my breasts, I bring you something.

I am like a little frightened hen....I know not whether I dare tell you.... My heart beats as though I would die.... It is a veil that I bring you.

A veil and the ribbons from my legs. You see: there is blood. By Apollo, it was in spite of me! I defended myself well; but the man who loves is stronger than we.

Wash them well; spare neither the salt nor the chalk. I will place four oboli for you at the feet of Aphrodite; even a drachma of silver.

XXXVI
SONG

WHEN he returned, I hid my face with my two hands. He said to me: "Fear nothing. Who has seen our kissing?—Who has seen us? The night and the moon.

"And the stars and the first dawn. The moon has mirrored herself in the lake and has told it to the water under the willows. The water of the lake has told it to the oar.

"And the oar has told it to the boat and the boat has told it to the fisher. Alas! Alas! If that were all! But the fisher has told it to a woman.

"The fisher has told it to a woman. My father and my mother and my sisters and all Hellas will know it."

XXXVII
BILITIS

ONE woman envelops herself in white wool. Another clothes herself in silk and gold. Another covers herself with flowers, with green leaves and with grapes.

As for me, I live only when I am naked. My lover, take me as I am, without robe or jewels or sandals. Here is Bilitis, quite alone.

My hair is black with its own blackness and my lips are red of their own color. My locks float about me, free and round, like feathers.

Take me as my mother made me in a night of love long past; and, if I please thee so, forget not to tell me.

XXXVIII
THE LITTLE HOUSE

THE little house where he has his bed is the prettiest in the world. It is made from the branches of trees, four walls of dried earth and a roof of thatch.

I love it, for there we have slept since the nights have grown cold; and, as the nights become still colder, they become longer also. When the day comes, I am very tired.

The mattress lies upon the ground; two covers of black wool shut in our bodies which warm each other. His chest presses against my breasts. My heart throbs. . . .

He embraces me so vigorously that he bruises me, poor little girl that I am; but when he is within me I know nothing more of the world, and my four limbs could be cut off without awakening me from my delight.

XXXIX
THE LOST LETTER

ALAS for me! I have lost his letter. I had placed it between my skin and my strophion, under the warmth of my breasts. I ran; it must have fallen.

I will retrace my steps; if someone has found it, they will read it to my mother and I shall be whipped before my jeering sisters.

If it is a man who has found it, he will return it to me; or even if he wishes to talk to me in secret, I will know how to charm it from him.

If it is a woman who has read it, O Guardian Zeus protect me! For she will tell it to all the world or she will take away my lover.

XL
SONG

" THE night is so profound that it penetrates my eyes.—Thou wilt not see the road. Thou wilt lose thyself in the forest."

"The noise of falling waters fills my ears.—Thou wouldst not hear the voice of thy lover were he but twenty steps away."

"The perfume of the flowers is so powerful that I shall faint and fall.—Thou wouldst not feel him even if he crossed thy path."

"Ah! He is very far from here, on the other side of the mountain; but I see him and I hear him and I feel him as though he touched me."

XLI
THE OATH

"When the water of the river mounts to the snow-hidden summits: when barley and wheat are sown in the moving furrows of the sea:

"When the pines grow from the lakes and water-lilies from the rocks: when the sun becomes black, when the moon falls upon the grass:

"Then, but only then, will I take another woman and forget thee, Bilitis, soul of my life, heart of my heart."

He has said that to me; he has said that to me! What matters the rest of the world; where art thou, boundless happiness which can compare with my happiness!

XLII
THE NIGHT

It is now I who search for him. Each night, very softly, I leave the house and I go by a long path to his meadow to see him sleeping.

Sometimes I remain for a long time without speaking, happy merely in seeing him, and I approach my lips to his and kiss only his breath.

Then, suddenly, I stretch myself upon him. He awakens in my arms, and he cannot rise, for I struggle. He gives up, and laughs, and clasps me. Thus we play in the night.

...First dawn,[8] O wicked light, thou already! In what ever-darkened cave, on what subterranean meadow, can we love so long that we lose remembrance of thee....

XLIII
CRADLE SONG

Sleep: I have sent to Sardis for thy toys, and for thy vestments to Babylon. Sleep: thou art the daughter of Bilitis and a king of the rising sun.

This wood is the palace which was built for thee alone and which I have given to thee. The trunks of the pines[9] are the columns; the high branches are the arches.

Sleep. That he may not awaken thee, I will sell the sun to the sea. The breeze from the wings of a dove is no lighter than thy breath.

Daughter of mine, flesh of my flesh, when thou openest thine eyes, say whether thou wishest the plain or the city or the mountain or the moon or the white cortège of the gods.

XLIV

THE TOMB OF THE NAIADS

THROUGH the woods covered with hoarfrost, I walked; my hair before my mouth glistened with little icicles, and my sandals were heavy with muddy cakes of snow.

He said to me: "What seekest thou?—I follow the tracks of a satyr. His little cloven steps alternate like holes in a white mantle." He said to me: "The satyrs are dead.

"The satyrs and the nymphs also. For thirty years there has been no winter so terrible. The track thou seest is that of a buck. Let us pause here, where their tomb is."

And, with the iron of his hoe, he broke the ice of the spring where once laughed the naiads. He lifted the great, frozen pieces and peered through them, toward the pale sky.

II
ELEGIACS AT MYTILENE

II. ELEGIACS AT MYTILENE

Εὐμορφοτέρα Μνασιδίκα τᾶς ἀπαλᾶς Γυρινῶς.

SAPPHO [10]

➤➤➤ ◄◄◄

XLV
TO THE VESSEL

BEAUTIFUL ship that has brought me here, along the shores of Ionia, I abandon thee to the glistening waves and, with a light foot, I leap upon the beach.

Thou wilt return to the country where the virgin is the friend of the nymphs. Forget not to thank those invisible counselors, and to carry them, as an offering, this branch plucked by my hands.

Thou wert once a pine and, on the mountains, the vast hot Notos shook thy branches with their squirrels and birds.

Let Boreos be now thy guide and push thee gently toward the port, black ship, escorted by dolphins, at the will of the kindly sea.

XLVI
PSAPPHA

I RUB my eyes ... I believe it is already day. Ah! Who is this near me? ... A woman? ... By Paphia, I had forgotten. ... O Charites! how I am shamed.

To what country am I come, and what is this island where love is understood thus? [11] If I were not so wearied, I would believe it a dream. ... Is it possible this may be Psappha? [1]

She sleeps... She is certainly beautiful, although her hair is cut like that of an athlete.[1] But this astonishing countenance, this virile breast, and these narrow hips. ...

I would like to go before she awakens. Alas! I am against the wall. I must step over her. I am afraid lest I touch her hip and that she will take me as I pass.

XLVII
THE DANCE OF GLOTTIS AND KYSE

T w o little girls carried me away to their house and, with the door firmly closed, they lit, at the fire, the wick of a lamp, and wished to dance for me.

Their cheeks were not painted and were brown as their little bellies. They pulled each other by the arms and talked at the same time in an agony of gaiety.

Seated on a mattress raised upon two trestles, Glottis sang in a sharp voice and struck the measures with her sonorous little hands.

Kyse danced shakily, then stopped, suffocated with laughter, took her sister by the breasts, bit her on the shoulder and overthrew her like a goat which wishes to play.

XLVIII
COUNSELS

T H E N Syllikmas entered and, seeing us so familiar, seated herself upon the bench. She took Glottis upon one knee, Kyse on the other, and said:

"Come here, little one." But I remained away. She resumed: "Art thou afraid of us? Approach: these children love thee. They will teach thee something thou knowest not: the honey of a woman's caresses.

"Man is violent and lazy. Doubtless thou knowest this. Avoid him. He has a flat chest, a rough skin, short hair, shaggy arms. But women are altogether beautiful.

"Women alone know how to love. Stay with us, Bilitis, stay. And if thou hast an ardent soul, thou wilt see thy beauty, as in a mirror, upon the bodies of the women thou lovest."

XLIX
UNCERTAINTY

I K N O W not whether I should espouse Glottis or Kyse. As they are not like each other, one would not console me for the other, and I fear lest I choose badly.

Each holds one of my hands and one of my breasts also. But to which shall I give my mouth? To which shall I give my heart and all that one cannot divide?

It is shameful to remain thus, all three in the same house. They talk of it in Mytilene. Yesterday, before the temple of Ares, a woman who passed did not say: "Greeting."

It is Glottis whom I prefer; but I cannot reject Kyse. What would become of her, all alone? Shall I leave them as they were and shall I take another friend?

L

THE MEETING

I HAVE found her, like a treasure, in a field, under a bush of myrtle, enveloped from throat to feet in a yellow peplos broidered with blue.

"I have no friend," she said; "for the nearest city is forty stadia from here. I live alone with my mother, who is a widow and always sad. If thou wishest, I will follow thee.

"I will follow thee to thy house, though it be at the other side of the island, and I will live with thee until thou sendest me away. Thy hand is tender and thine eyes are blue.

"Let us go. I carry nothing with me but this little naked Astarte which hangs from my necklace. We will put it near thine and we will give them roses in recompense for each night."

LI

THE LITTLE TERRA-COTTA ASTARTE

THE little guardian Astarte which protects Mnasidika was modeled at Camiros by a skilful potter. She is large as a thumb and of fine yellow earth.

Her hair falls back and curls upon her narrow shoulders. Her eyes are cut very long and her mouth is very small. For she is the Most-Beautiful.

With her right hand she points to her delta which is worked with little holes on the lower belly and along the groins. For she is the Most-Amorous-One.

With her left arm, she supports her heavy, rounded breasts. Between her wide hips protrudes a fecund belly. For she is the Mother-Of-All-Things.

LII
DESIRE

S h e entered and, passionately, her eyes half closed, she united her lips with mine and our tongues touched each other. . . . Never was there in my life a kiss like that one.

She stood against me, all love and consentment. One of my knees, little by little, gave way as though for a lover.

My hand wandered over her tunic, seeking to divine the hidden body which, by turns, undulating, yielded or, arching, stiffened with shiverings of the skin.

With her eyes in delirium, she pointed toward the bed; but we had not the right to love before the ceremony of wedding, and we separated brusquely.

LIII
THE WEDDING

I n the morning they had the wedding feast [12] at the house of Acalanthis whom she had adopted for a mother. Mnasidika wore the white veil and I the male tunic.

Then, amidst twenty women, she put on her robes of festival. Perfumed with bakkaris, sifted with powder of gold, her cool and animated skin attracted furtive hands.

In her chamber filled with foliage, she waited for me like a spouse. And I carried her away on a chariot between myself and the nymphagogue. One of her little breasts burned in my hand.

They chanted the nuptial song; the flutes played also. I carried Mnasidika under the shoulders and under the knees, and we crossed the rose-covered threshold.

LIV
THE PAST WHICH SURVIVES

I w i l l leave the bed as she has left it, unmade and rumpled, the covers tangled, so that the form of her body may remain impressed beside mine.

Until tomorrow, I will not go to the bath, I will not wear any garments, I will not comb my hair, for fear lest I efface her caresses.

This morning, I will not eat, nor this evening; and upon my lips

I will place neither rouge nor powder, in order that her kiss may remain.

I will leave the shutters closed and I will not open the door, for fear lest the remembrance which she has left might fly out upon the wind.

LV

METAMORPHOSIS

FORMERLY I was amorous of the beauty of young men and the remembrance of their words kept me awake.

I remember having graven a name in the bark of a plane tree. I remember having left a strip of my tunic in a path where someone would pass.

I remember having loved ... O Pannychis, my babe, in what hands have I left thee? How, O unfortunate one, have I abandoned thee!

Today and forever, Mnasidika alone possesses me. May she receive, as a sacrifice, the happiness of those whom I have deserted for her.

LVI

THE NAMELESS TOMB

MNASIDIKA took me by the hand and led me outside the gates of the city, to a little uncultivated field where there was a marble stele. And she said: "This was the lover of my mother."

Then I felt a great shiver and, still holding her by the hand, I leaned upon her shoulder in order to read the four lines between the broken cup and the serpent:

"It is not death which has carried me away, but the Nymphs of the fountains. I rest here under the light earth with the severed hair of Xantho. Let her alone weep for me. I tell not my name."

For a long time we remained standing, and we did not pour a libation. For how could we call an unknown soul from the throngs of Hades?

LVII

THE THREE BEAUTIES OF MNASIDIKA

So that Mnasidika may be protected by the gods, I have sacrificed to the Aphrodite-Who-Loves-The-Smiles, two male hares and two doves.

And I have sacrificed to Ares two cocks armed for fighting, and to sinister Hekate two dogs that howled under the knife.

And it is not without reason that I have implored these three immortals, for Mnasidika carries on her countenance the reflection of their triple divinity.

Her lips are red like copper, her hair bluish like iron, and her eyes black like silver.

LVIII
THE CAVE OF THE NYMPHS

T H Y feet are more delicate than those of silvery Thetis. Between thy crossed arms thou unitest thy breasts, cradling them softly like the bodies of two beautiful doves.

Beneath thy hair thou dissemblest thy moist eyes, thy trembling mouth and the pink flowers of thine ears; but nothing stops my regard nor the warm breath of my kiss.

For, in the secret of thy body, it is thou, Mnasidika, beloved, who hidest the Cave of the Nymphs [13] of which old Homer spoke: the place where the naiads weave their purple linens:

The place where glide, drop by drop, the inexhaustible springs, and where the gate of the North lets men descend and the gate of the South lets immortals enter.

LIX
MNASIDIKA'S BREASTS

C A R E F U L L Y , with one hand, she opened her tunic and offered me her warm, sweet breasts, as one would offer to the goddess a pair of living turtle-doves.

"Love them well," she said to me. "I love them so much! They are cherished, little children. I busy myself with them when I am alone. I play with them; I give them pleasure.

"I douche them with milk. I powder them with flowers. My soft hair, which dries them, is dear to their little points. I caress them, and shiver. I enfold them in wool.

"Because I shall never have children, be their nursling, my love; and, because they are so far from my mouth, give them kisses for me."

LX
THE DOLL

I H A V E given her a doll, a doll of wax with rosy cheeks. Its arms are attached by little pegs and even its legs can move.

When we are together, she couches it between us and it is our child. In the evening she cradles it and gives it the breast before putting it to sleep.

She has woven it three little tunics and we gave it jewels on the day of the Aphrodisian Festival; jewels and flowers also.

She watches over its virtue and will not let it go out without her; not in the sun, above all, for the little doll would melt into drops of wax.

LXI
TENDERNESSES

CLOSE thine arms; gently, like a girdle about me. O touch, touch my skin thus! Neither water nor the breeze of noontide are so soft as thy hand.

Today, cherish me, little sister; it is thy turn. Remember thou the tendernesses which I taught thee in the night past, and kneel thou near me, silently, for I am weary.

Thy lips descend upon my lips. All thine unbound hair follows them like a caress after a kiss. It glides over my left breast, it hides thine eyes from me.

Give me thy hand; it is hot. Press mine; hold it always. Hands better than mouths unite, and their passion is equaled by nothing.

LXII
GAMES

MORE than her toys or her doll, I am a play-thing for her. With all parts of my body, she amuses herself like a child, through the long hours, without speaking.

She loosens my hair and reforms it according to her caprice, knotting it under my chin like a thick cloth, or twisting it upon the nape of my neck, or braiding it to the end.

She regards with astonishment the color of my lashes, the fold of my elbow. Sometimes she makes me kneel and place my hands upon the rugs.

Then (it is one of her games) she slips her little head underneath and imitates the trembling kid which sucks from the belly of its mother.

LXIII

PENUMBRA

U N D E R N E A T H the cover of transparent wool, we slipped, she and I. Even our heads were covered, and the lamp illumined the cloth above us.

Thus I saw her dear body in a mysterious light. We were very near, one to the other, more free, more intimate, more naked. "In the same chiton," she said.

We had left our hair bound up in order to be still more uncovered, and in the close air of the bed, the odors of two women ascended, of two natural cassolettes.

Nothing in the world, not even the lamp, saw us that night. Which of us was loved, she alone, and I, could say. But the men shall know nothing of it.

LXIV

THE SLEEPER

S H E sleeps in her unbound hair, her hands joined behind her neck. Does she dream? Her mouth is open; she breathes gently.

With a bit of white swan's-down, I wipe away the perspiration of her arms, the fever of her cheeks, but without awakening her. Her closed eyelids are two blue flowers.

Very softly, I will arise; I will go draw water, milk the cow and ask fire of the neighbors. I would arrange my hair and dress before she opens her eyes.

Sleep, dwell for long between her fair, curved eyelids, and continue the happy night with a dream of good augury.

LXV

THE KISS

I W I L L kiss, from one end to the other, the long dark waves spreading from thy neck, O sweet bird, captive dove, whose heart bounds beneath my hand.

I will take thy lips within my lips as an infant takes the breast of its mother. Shudder! ... for the kiss penetrates deeply and suffices love.

I will move my tongue lightly along thine arms and upon thy neck; and I will wind along thy tender sides the lengthening caress of my nails.

Hear, roaring in thine ears, all the rumor of the sea ... Mnasidika! Thy look makes me suffer. Like thy lips, I would enclose thy
burning eyelids with my kiss.

LXVI
JEALOUS CARE

D o not arrange thy hair, for fear lest the over-heated iron burn thy
neck or thy locks. Leave it upon thy shoulders and spread over thine
arms.

Do not dress thyself, for fear lest the girdle redden the slender
folds of thy hips. Remain naked, like a little girl.

Do not ever rise, for fear lest thy tender feet be injured in walking. Remain in the bed, O victim of Eros, and I will dress thy poor
wound.

For I would not see upon thy body other marks, Mnasidika, than
the stain of a prolonged kiss, the scratch of a sharp nail, or the redden-
ing bar of my embrace.

LXVII
THE DISTRACTED EMBRACE

L o v e me, not with smiles, flutes, or woven flowers, but with thy
heart and thy tears, as I love thee with my breast and my lamentations.

When thy breasts alternate with my breasts, when I feel thy
life touching my life, when thy knees draw up behind me, then my
panting mouth knows not how more to unite with thine.

Clasp me as I clasp thee! See, the lamp has died out; we roll
about in the night; but I press thy moving body and I hear thy perpetual plaint. ...

Moan! moan! moan! O woman! Eros leads us in sorrow. Thou
wilt suffer less on the bed in bringing a child into the world than when
giving birth to thy love.

LXVIII
THE HEART

P a n t i n g, I take her hand and press it against the moist skin of
my left breast. And I turn my head here and there and I move my
lips without speaking.

My disordered heart, abrupt and hard, beats and beats in my breast as an imprisoned satyr would knock, imprisoned in a leathern bottle. She says to me: "Thy heart makes thee ill...."

"O Mnasidika," I respond, "The heart of a woman is not there. That is only a poor bird, a dove which stirs its feeble wings. The heart of a woman is more terrible.

"Like a little myrtle berry, it burns with a red flame and under an abundant foam. It is there that I feel myself bitten by voracious Aphrodite."

LXIX
WORDS IN THE NIGHT

W E rest, our eyes closed: the silence is deep about our couch. Ineffable nights of summer! But she, believing me asleep, lays her warm hand upon my arm.

She murmurs: "Bilitis, thou sleepest?" My heart throbs, but, without response, I respire regularly like a woman couched in dreams. Then she begins to speak:

"Because thou hearest me not," she says, "Ah! How I love thee." And she repeats my name: "Bilitis... Bilitis...." And she touches me with the tips of her trembling fingers.

"It is mine, this mouth! Mine alone! Is there another so beautiful in the world? Ah! My happiness, my happiness! Mine are these naked arms, this neck, this hair...."

LXX
ABSENCE

S H E has gone out, she is far away, but I see her, for all things in this chamber are full of her, all belong to her, and I, like the rest.

This bed, still warm, over which I let my mouth stray, is impressed with the form of her body. On this soft pillow has lain her little head enveloped in her hair.

This is the basin in which she has bathed, this comb has penetrated the knots of her tangled hair. These slippers have received her naked feet. These pockets of gauze have enclosed her breasts.

But that which I dare not touch with my finger is the mirror in which she has seen her fiery bruises and in which, perhaps, still exists the reflection of her moist lips.

LXXI
LOVE

ALAS! If I think of her, my throat becomes dry,[14] my head droops, my breasts harden and pain me, I shiver and I weep as I walk.

If I see her, my heart stops, my hands tremble, my feet grow cold, a blush of fire mounts to my cheeks, my temples throb grievously.

If I touch her, I become mad, my arms stiffen, my knees falter. I fall before her and lie like a woman about to die.

Whenever she speaks to me, I am wounded. Her love is a torture and the passers-by hear my plaints.... Alas! How can I call her Well-Belovèd?

LXXII
PURIFICATION

THERE thou art! Take off thy ribbons and thy clasps and thy tunic. Remove even thy sandals, even the ribbons from thy legs, even the band from thy breast.

Wash the black from thine eyebrows and the red from thy lips. Efface the white from thy shoulders and uncurl thy hair in the water.

For I would have thee all pure as thou wert born upon the bed at the feet of thy fecund mother and before thy proud father.

So chaste that my hand in thy hand will make thee blush even to thy lips and one word of mine in thine ear will enflame thy wandering eyes.

LXXIII
THE CRADLE OF MNASIDIKA

MY little child, though I may have so few years more than thee, I love thee, not as a lover but as though thou hadst come forth from my laboring entrails.

When, stretched upon my knees, thy two frail arms about me, thou seekest my breast, thy mouth clinging, pressing my nipples slowly between thy palpitating lips:

Then I dream that, in former times, I truly nursed this delicate mouth, supple and moist, this vase of crimson murrhine in which the happiness of Bilitis is mysteriously enclosed.

Sleep. I will cradle thee with one hand upon my knee which

rocks thee. Sleep so. I will sing for thee little mournful songs which bring sleep to the newly-born.

LXXIV
A WALK BY THE SEA

As we were walking upon the shore, without speaking and enveloped to the chin in our robes of sombre wool, joyous young girls passed by.

"Ah! It is Bilitis and Mnasidika! See the pretty little squirrel we have caught; it is soft as a bird and timid as a rabbit.

"At Lydia's house we will put it in a cage and give it plenty of milk with lettuce leaves. It is a female; she will live a long time."

And the care-free ones departed, running. As for us, without speaking we seated ourselves, I upon a rock, she upon the sand, and we gazed at the sea.

LXXV
THE OBJECT

"Greeting, Bilitis, Mnasidika, greeting.—Be seated. How is thy husband?—Too well. Do not tell him that you have seen me. He would slay me if he knew I had been here. Have no fear."

"And this is your chamber? And this your bed? Pardon me: I am curious.—Thou knowest, however, the bed of Myrrhina.—So little.—It is said to be pretty.—And lascivious. Oh my dear! But we conceal it."

"What wishest thou of me?—That thou lend me . . .—Speak.— I dare not name the object.[15]—We do not have one.—Truly?—Mnasidika is a virgin.—Then where can one buy it?—From the harness-maker, Drakon."

"Tell me also where thou buyest thy thread for embroidery. Mine breaks if one looks at it.—I make it myself, but that which Nais sells is excellent.—At what price?—Three oboli.—It is dear. And the object?—Two drachmæ.—Farewell."

LXXVI
EVENING NEAR THE FIRE

The winter is hard, Mnasidika. All is frozen except our bed. But arise and come with me, for I have lit a great fire with dead branches and broken wood.

We will warm ourselves, crouching quite naked, our hair ever our backs, and we will drink milk from the same cup and we will eat cakes with honey.

How gay and noisy the flame is! Art thou not too near? Thy skin reddens. Let me kiss it wherever the fire has burned it.

Amidst the ardent firebrands, I will heat the iron and I will dress thy hair here. With a dead ember I will write thy name upon the wall.

LXXVII
ENTREATIES

WHAT dost thou wish? Say. If it is necessary, I will sell my last jewels so that an attentive slave may wait upon the desire of thine eyes and every thirst of thy lips.

If the milk of our goats seems insipid to thee, I will hire for thee, as for an infant, a nurse with swollen breasts who will suckle thee each morning.

If our bed seems rough to thee, I will buy all the soft cushions, all the coverlets of silk, all the feather-woven cloths, of the Amathusian merchants.

All. But I should suffice thee; and though we slept upon the earth, thou shouldst find it softer than the warm bed of a stranger.

LXXVIII
THE EYES

GREAT eyes of Mnasidika, how happy you make me when love darkens your lids and quickens you and shadows you with tears.

But how maddened, when you turn elsewhere, distracted by a woman who passes or by a remembrance which is not mine.

Then my cheeks hollow themselves, my hands tremble, and I suffer.... Before you, life seems to leave all my members.

Great eyes of Mnasidika, cease not to regard me, or I will pierce you with my needle and then you will see only the terrible night.

LXXIX
FARDS

ALL, all my life, and the world, and the men: all that is not of her is nothing. All that is not of her, I give to thee, passer-by.

Does she know the labors I accomplish to be fair in her eyes, with my hair and with my fards, with my robes and my perfumes?

As long a time I would turn a mill-stone, I would wield an oar or dig in the earth, if it were a necessary price to retain her here.

But may she never know, Goddesses who watch over us. The day on which she learns that I love her, she will seek another woman.

LXXX
THE SILENCE OF MNASIDIKA

S H E had laughed all the day, and she even had mocked me a little. She had refused to obey me before many strange women.

When we returned, I affected not to speak to her, and as she cast herself upon my neck, saying: "Thou art offended?" I said to her:

"Ah! Thou art no longer as formerly, thou art no longer as on the first day. I no longer recognize thee, Mnasidika." She did not respond to me.

But she put on all the jewels which she had not worn for a long time, and the same yellow robe, broidered with blue, as on the day of our meeting.

LXXXI
SCENE

"W H E R E wert thou?—At the flower-merchant's. I bought some very beautiful irises. Here they are, I have brought them to thee.—In so long a time thou hast bought four flowers?—The merchant-woman detained me.

"Thy cheeks are pale and thine eyes brilliant.—It is fatigue from the walk.—Thy hair is moist [16] and tangled.—It is the heat and the wind which blew down my hair.

"Someone has untied thy girdle. I made the knot myself, looser than this one.—So loose that it became undone; a slave who was passing retied it for me.

"There is a spot upon thy robe.—It is water which has fallen from the flowers.—Mnasidika, my little soul, thine irises are fairer than any in all Mytilene.—That I know well; that I know well."

LXXXII
WAITING

T H E sun has passed all the night among the dead, while I have waited, seated upon my bed, weary from watching. The wick of the exhausted lamp has burned to the end.

She will not return; there is the last star. I know well that she will not return. I know even the name that I hate. Nevertheless, I still wait.

If she might come now! Yes, if she might come, her hair disordered and without roses, her robe soiled, spotted, rumpled, her tongue dry and her eyelids black!

When she opened the door, I would say to her . . . but here she is. . . . This is her robe that I touch, her hands, her hair, her skin! I kiss her with distracted lips and I weep.

LXXXIII
SOLITUDE

F o r whom, now, shall I fard my lips? [17] For whom shall I polish my nails? For whom shall I perfume my hair?

For whom are my breasts powdered with rouge, if they no longer tempt her? For whom are my arms laved with milk, if they may never more embrace her?

How can I sleep? How can I lie upon the bed? This evening, my hand, in all my bed, could not find her warm hand.

I dare not return to my house, to the chamber so frightfully empty. I dare not reopen the door. I dare not even reopen mine eyes.

LXXXIV
A LETTER

I t is impossible, impossible. I pray thee upon my knees, with tears, all the tears I have wept over this horrible letter, not to abandon me thus.

Consider thou how terrible it is to lose thee forever for a second time, after having had the great joy of hoping to reconquer thee. Ah! My love! Thou knowest not to what point I have adored thee!

Hear me. Consent to see me once more. Wilt thou be, tomorrow, at sunset, before thy door? Tomorrow, or the day following? I will come to take thee. Do not refuse me this.

The last time, perhaps; be it so; but once more, this once more! I demand it of thee, I beg it of thee. Reflect that, upon thy reply, the rest of my life depends.

LXXXV
THE ATTEMPT

T H O U wert jealous of us, Gyrinno, too ardent girl. How many garlands didst thou suspend from the knocker of our door! Thou didst wait for us in the passage and thou didst follow us in the streets.

Now thou art, according to thy vows, extended upon the loved place and thy head is upon the pillow about which floats the odor of another woman. Thou art larger than she was. Thy different body startles me.

See! I have yielded at last. Yes, it is I. Thou mayest play with my breasts, caress my belly, open my knees. All my body surrenders to thy tireless lips—Alas!

Ah! Gyrinno! With love my tears also overflow. Wipe them with thy hair; do not kiss them, my dear; and enlace me closer yet, to still my tremblings.

LXXXVI
THE EFFORT

A G A I N! Enough of sighs and of outstretched arms! Recommence! Thinkest thou, then, that love is a recreation? Gyrinno, it is a task, and of all the most rude.

Awaken, thou! Thou shalt not sleep! What care I for thy blue eyelids and the bar of pain which burns thy thin legs! Astarte seethes in my loins.

We entered our couch before twilight. Behold already the wicked dawn; but I am not wearied with so little. I will not sleep before the second evening.

I will not sleep; nor shalt thou sleep. Oh! How bitter is the taste of morning! Appreciate it, Gyrinno. The embraces are more difficult, but stranger and softer.

LXXXVII
TO GYRINNO

T H I N K not that I have loved thee. I have eaten thee like a ripe fig, I have drunk thee like an ardent water, I have carried thee about me like a girdle of skin.

I have amused myself with thy body, because thou hast short

hair, pointed breasts upon thy lean chest, and nipples black like two little dates.

Like water and fruits, a woman also is necessary; but already I no longer know thy name, thou who hast passed through my arms like the shadow of another adored one.

Between thy flesh and mine, a burning dream has possessed me. I pressed thee upon me as upon a wound, and I cried: "Mnasidika! Mnasidika! Mnasidika!"

LXXXVIII
THE LAST ESSAY

"WHAT wishest thou, old woman?—To console thee.—It is useless trouble.—They have told me that since thy separation, thou goest from love to love, finding no forgetfulness nor peace. I have come to offer thee someone.

"Speak.—It is a young slave, born at Sardis. She has no equal in the world, for she is at the same time man and woman, although her chest, her long hair and her clear voice produce the illusion.

"Her age?—Sixteen years.—Her stature?—Tall. She has known no one here except Psappha who loves her desperately and would buy her of me for twenty minæ. If thou wilt hire her, she is thine.—And what should I do with her?

"Behold, for twenty-two nights I have essayed in vain to escape from memory. . . . Be it so; I will take this one more. But warn the poor little one, that she be not frightened if I sob in her arms."

LXXXIX
THE WOUNDING MEMORY

I REMEMBER . . . (at what hour of the day is it not before my eyes!) I remember the manner in which She lifted her hair with her pale, slender fingers.

I remember one night which she passed, her cheek upon my breast, so softly that happiness held me awake; and on the day following she had upon her face the mark of my rounded nipple.

I see her holding her cup of milk and regarding me sideways, with a smile. I see her, powdered, her hair dressed, opening her great eyes before her mirror and retouching with her finger the red of her lips.

And, above all, if my despair is a perpetual torture, it is because

I know, moment by moment, how she swoons in the arms of another, what she demands of her and what she gives her.

XC
TO THE WAX DOLL

DOLL of wax, dear plaything which she called her child, she left thee also, and she has forgotten thee like myself who, with her, was thy father or thy mother, I know not which.

The pressure of her lips has faded thy little cheeks; and here, on thy left hand, is the broken finger which made her weep so much. This little cyclas which thou wearest, it was she who broidered it for thee.

She said thou couldst already read. Nevertheless, thou wert not weaned and, in the evening, bending over thee, she would open her tunic and give thee the breast, "so that thou wouldst not cry," she would say.

Doll, if I wished to see her again, I would give thee to Aphrodite, as the dearest of my gifts. But I wish to think that she is wholly dead.

XCI
FUNEREAL CHANT

SING a funereal chant, Muses of Mytilene, sing! The earth is sombre like a vestment of mourning and the yellow trees quiver like severed hair.

Heraïos! O sweet and sorrowful month! The leaves fall gently like snow; the sun penetrates more deeply into the thinning forest. . . . I hear nothing more, but the silence.

Behold, they have carried Pittakos, laden with years, to the tomb. Many whom I knew are dead. And she who lives is to me as though she were no longer.

This is the tenth autumn I have seen dying upon this plain. It is time I also vanished away. Weep with me, Muses of Mytilene; weep upon my steps!

III
EPIGRAMS IN THE ISLE OF KYPROS

III. EPIGRAMS IN THE ISLE OF KYPROS

Ἀλλά με ναρκίσοις ἀναδήσατε, καὶ πλαγιαύλων
γεύσατε καὶ κροκίνοις χρίσατε γυῖα μύροις.
Καὶ Μυτιληναίῳ τὸν πνεύμονα τέγξατε Βάκχῳ
καὶ συζεύξατε μοι ψωλάδα παρθενικήν.

PHILODEMOS [18]

➤➤➤ ◄◄◄

XCII
HYMN TO ASTARTE

MOTHER inexhaustible, incorruptible, creatrix, first-born, self-engendered, self-conceived, issue of thyself alone and rejoicing in thyself: Astarte!

O perpetually fecund, O virgin and nurse of all, chaste and lascivious, pure and fruitive, ineffable, nocturnal, soft, breather of fire, foam of the sea!

Thou who accordest favors in secret, thou who unitest, thou who lovest, thou who possessest in furious desire the multiple races of savage beasts and joinest the sexes in the forests!

O Astarte, irresistible, hear me, take me, possess me, O moon; and, thirteen times each year, draw from my entrails the libation of my blood!

XCIII
HYMN TO THE NIGHT

THE black masses of the trees are immovable as the mountains. The stars fill the vast sky. A warm breeze like a human breath caresses my eyes and my cheeks.

O Night, who gavest birth to the Gods! How sweet thou art upon my lips! How warm thou art in my hair! How thou enterest into me now, and how I feel myself pregnant with all thy springtime!

The flowers that shall blossom shall all be born of me. The

wind which respires is my breath; the perfume which passes is my desire. All the stars are in mine eyes.

Thy voice: is it the roar of the sea? Is it the silence of the plain? Thy voice: I comprehend it not, but it bends my head to the ground, and my tears lave my two hands.

XCIV
THE MENADES

THROUGH the forests that dominate the sea, the Menades hurtled. Maskale, with hot breasts, shrieked, brandishing the phallos of sycamore smeared with vermilion.

All, under their bassaris skins and their crowns of vine branches, ran and cried and leapt, the krotales clapping in their hands and the thyrsi [19] cracking the skins of the resounding drums.

With wetted hair, agile legs, reddened and crowding breasts, sweating cheeks, foaming lips, O Dionysos, they offered thee again the love thou didst cast within them.

And the wind of the sea lifted toward the sky the ruddy hair of Helikomis, twisting it like a furious flame upon a torch of white wax.

XCV
THE SEA OF KYPRIS

ON the highest promontory, I stretched myself out. The sea was dark as a field of violets. The milky-way gushed out from the great divine breast.

A thousand Menades slept about me in the mangled flowers. The long grasses mingled with their hair. And then, behold, the sun was born from the waters of the East.

They were the same waters and the same shores that, one day, saw appear the white body of Aphrodite.... Suddenly, I hid my eyes in my hands.

For I had seen, trembling upon the water, a thousand tiny lips of light: the pure sex or the smile of Kypris Philommeïdes.

XCVI
THE PRIESTESSES OF ASTARTE

THE priestesses of Astarte make love at the rising of the moon; then they arise and bathe in a vast basin with a marge of silver.

With their curved fingers, they comb their hair; and their hands, tinted with crimson, blended with their black curls, seem like branches of coral in a sombre and undulating sea.

They never depilate themselves, so that the triangle of the Goddess marks their belly as on a temple; but they paint themselves with brushes and perfume themselves deeply.

The priestesses of Astarte make love at the setting of the moon; then, in a carpeted hall where burns a tall, gold lamp, they stretch themselves out at random.

XCVII
THE MYSTERIES

W I T H I N the thrice-mysterious enclosure where the men never enter, we made a festival for thee, Astarte of the Night, Mother of the World, Fountain of the Life of the Gods!

I will reveal something, but not more than is permitted. About a Phallos crowned, an hundred women rocked, shrieking. The initiates were in men's vestments, the others in divided tunics.

The smoke of perfumes, the fumes of torches, wavered between us like clouds. I wept burning tears. All, at the feet of the Berbeia, we cast ourselves upon our backs.

At last, when the religious Act was consummated and when, into the Unique Triangle, had been plunged the crimson Phallos, the mystery commenced; but I will tell no more.

XCVIII
THE EGYPTIAN COURTESANS

I H A V E been, with Plango, among the Egyptian courtesans, at the highest part of the old city. They have amphoras of earth, plates of copper, and yellow matting where they squat without effort.

Their chambers are silent, without angles and without corners, so much their successive coatings of blue lime have blunted the pillars and rounded the base of the walls.

They sit motionless, their hands resting on their knees. When they offer food, they murmur: "Happiness." And when one thanks them, they say: "Grace to thee."

They understand Hellenic but feign to speak it badly so as to laugh at us in their own tongue; but we, (a tooth for a tooth) we speak Lydian and they are suddenly uneasy.

XCIX
I SING OF MY FLESH AND MY LIFE

S u r e l y I shall not sing of celebrated lovers. If they are no more, why speak of them? Am I not like them? Have I not enough to think of in myself?

I will forget thee, Pasiphaë, although thy passion was extreme. I will not praise thee, Syrinx, nor thee, Byblis, nor thee, chosen among all by the Goddess, Helen of the white arms!

If anyone has suffered, I scarcely know it. If anyone has loved, I love more. I sing of my flesh and my life, and not of the sterile shadows of buried lovers.

Rest upon thy bed, O my body, according to thy voluptuous mission! Taste thy daily enjoyments and the passions without a to-morrow. Leave not a delight unknown to be regretted on the day of thy death.

C
THE PERFUMES

I w i l l perfume all my skin to attract lovers. Upon my fair legs, in a basin of silver, I will pour the spikenard of Tarsos and the metopion of Egypt.

Under my arms, crisp mint; upon my lashes and upon my eyes, sweet-marjoram of Kôs. Slave, loosen my hair and fill it with the smoke of incense.

Here is œnanthium from the mountains of Kypros; I will let it run between my breasts; this liquor of roses, which comes from Phaselis, shall perfume my neck and my cheeks.

And now, pour upon my loins the irresistible bakkaris. It is better, for a courtesan, to know the perfumes of Lydia than the ways of the Peloponnesos.

CI
CONVERSATION[20]

"G o o d morning.—Good morning, also.—Thou art in a great hurry.—Perhaps less than thou thinkest.—Thou art a pretty girl.—Perhaps more so than thou believest."

"What is thy charming name?—I do not tell that so quickly.—

Thou hast someone this evening?—Always the one who loves me. —And how dost thou love him?—As he wishes."

"Let us sup together.—If thou wishest it. But what wilt thou give?—This.—Five drachmæ? It is for my slave. And for me?— Say it thyself.—An hundred."

"Where livest thou?—In this blue house.—At what hour dost thou wish me to send for thee?—At once, if thou wishest.—At once. —Go before."

CII
THE TORN ROBE

" H o there! By the two goddesses, who is the insolent one who has put his foot upon my robe?—It is a lover.—It is a blockhead. —I have been awkward; pardon me."

"Imbecile! My yellow robe is all torn in the back, and if I walk thus in the street, they will take me for a poor girl who serves Kypris inversely."

"Wilt thou not stop?—I believe that he speaks to me again!— Why dost thou leave me, thus angered? . . . Thou respondest not? Alas! I dare speak no more."

"I certainly must return to my house to change my robe.—And may I not follow thee?—Who is thy father?—He is the wealthy ship-owner, Nikias.—Thou hast fine eyes; I pardon thee."

CIII
THE JEWELS

A DIADEM of fretted gold crowns my straight, white forehead. Five chains of gold which follow the curve of my cheeks and chin, are suspended from my hair by two large clasps.

Upon my arms, which Iris would envy, thirteen silver bracelets are ranged. How heavy they are! But they are weapons; and I know one enemy who has suffered from them.

I am truly all covered with gold. My breasts are cuirassed with two pectorals of gold. Even the images of the gods have not more riches than I.

And I wear over my heavy robe a girdle [21] worked with silver wire. There thou canst read this verse: "Love me eternally; but be not afflicted if I deceive thee three times each day."

CIV
INDIFFERENCE

WHEN he has entered my chamber, whoever he may be, (this matters nothing): "See," I say to my slave, "what a handsome man! And should not a courtesan be happy?"

I declare he is Adonis, Ares or Herakles, according to his countenance; or The Old Man of the Sea, if his hair is pale silver. And then what disdain for trifling youth!

"Ah!" I say, "If I had not to pay my florist and my goldsmith tomorrow, how I would love to say to thee: I do not wish thy gold! I am thy passionate servant!"

Then, when he has clasped his arms beneath my shoulders, I see a boatman [22] pass like a divine image over the starry sky of my transparent lids.

CV
PURE WATER OF THE BASIN

"PURE water of the basin, immobile mirror, tell me of my beauty. —Bilitis, or whoever thou art, Tethys perhaps, or Amphitrite, thou art beautiful, thou knowest.

"Thy face inclines beneath thy thick hair which is heavy with flowers and perfumes. Thy soft eyelids scarcely open, and thy flanks are weary from the movements of love.

"Thy body, fatigued with the weight of thy breasts, bears the fine marks of nails and the blue stains of the kiss. Thine arms are reddened from the embrace. Each line of thy skin was loved.

"Clear water of the basin, thy freshness brings repose. Receive me, who am truly wearied. Take away the fard of my cheeks and the sweat of my body and the remembrance of the night."

CVI
VOLUPTUOUSNESS

UPON a white terrace, in the night, they left us, swooning among the roses. Warm sweat ran like tears from our armpits, over our breasts. Overwhelming voluptuousness purpled our prostrate heads.

Four captive doves, bathed in four perfumes, fluttered above us in the silence. From their wings, drops of perfume fell upon the naked women. I was overrun with the essence of iris.

O lassitude! I rested my cheek upon the belly of a young girl who enveloped herself in the coolness of my moist hair. The perfume of her saffroned skin intoxicated my opened mouth. She closed her thighs about my neck.

I slept, but an exhausting dream awakened me; the iynx, bird of nocturnal desires, sang distractedly from afar. I coughed with a shiver. Little by little, a languishing arm like a flower raised itself in the air toward the moon.

CVII
THE INN

INNKEEPER, we are four. Give us a chamber and two beds. It is now too late to return to the city, and the rain has broken the road.

Bring a basket of figs, some cheese, and dark wine; but first remove my sandals and bathe my feet, for the mud tickles me.

Send to the chamber two basins with water, a full lamp, a krater and kylix. Shake thou the covers and beat the cushions.

But let the beds be of good maple and the planks noiseless! Tomorrow thou needst not awaken us.

CVIII
THE SERVANTS

FOUR slaves guard my house: two robust Thracians at my door, a Sicilian in my kitchen, and a docile and silent Phrygian woman for the service of my bed.

The two Thracians are handsome men. Each has a staff in his hand to chase away poor lovers and a hammer to nail upon the wall the garlands which are sent me.

The Sicilian is a rare cook; I paid twelve minæ for him. No one knows as he does how to prepare fried croquettes and cakes of poppy.

The Phrygian bathes me, dresses my hair and depilates me. She sleeps in the morning in my chamber, and, three times each month, she takes my place with my lovers.

CIX
THE BATH

CHILD, guard well the door and let no passer-by enter, for I and six girls with beautiful arms would bathe ourselves in secret in the warm water of the basin.

We wish only to laugh and swim. Let the lovers stay in the street. We will dip our legs in the water and, seated upon the marble brink, we will play with dice.

We will play also with the ball. Let no lovers enter; our hair is too wet, our throats have goose-flesh and the ends of our fingers are wrinkled.

Moreover, he would repent it, he who surprised us naked! Bilitis is not Athena,[23] but she shows herself only at her hours and chastises too ardent eyes.

CX
TO HER BREASTS

FLOWERS of flesh, O my breasts! How rich in voluptuousness you are! My breasts in my hands, how soft you are, how gently warm, how youthfully perfumed!

Formerly you were frozen like the breast of a statue and hard as the insensate marble. Since you have softened, I cherish you more, you who have been so loved.

Your sleek, rounded forms are the honor of my brown torso. Whether I imprison you in golden lace or whether I deliver you all naked, you precede me with your splendor.

Therefore, be happy, this night. If my fingers give forth caresses, you alone shall know them until tomorrow morning; for, this night, Bilitis has paid Bilitis.

CXI
MYDZOURIS

MYDZOURIS, little filth, weep not. Thou art. my friend. If the women insult thee again, it is I who will answer them. Come into my arms and dry thine eyes.

Yes, I know thou art a horrible child and that thy mother taught thee early to prove thy courage in all things. But thou art young and therefore thou canst do nothing that is not charming.

The mouth of a girl of fifteen remains pure in spite of all. The lips of a gray-haired woman, even if virgin, are degraded; for the only disgrace is to grow old and we are blemished only by wrinkles.

Mydzouris, I admire thy frank eyes, thine impudent and bold name, thy laughing voice and thy light body. Come to my house, thou shalt be my aid and, when we go out together, the women shall say to thee: "Greeting."

CXII
THE TRIUMPH OF BILITIS

I n the procession they carried me in triumph, me, Bilitis, all naked upon a car formed like a shell, into which slaves, during the night, had placed the blooms of ten thousand roses.

I reclined, my hands under my neck, my feet alone clad in gold, and my body outstretched softly upon the bed of my warm hair mingled with cool petals.

Twelve children, with wings on their shoulders, served me as a goddess; one of them held a shade, the others showered me with perfume or burned incense in the prow.

And all about me I heard rustling the ardent murmur of the multitude, while the breath of desire floated about my nudity in the blue fog of the aromatics.

CXIII
TO A GOD OF WOOD

O v e n e r a b l e Priapos, god of wood whom I have fastened in the marble border of my bath, it is not without reason, guardian of orchards, that thou art watching here over the courtesans.

God, we did not buy thee to sacrifice our virginities to thee. No one can give that which is no more, and the zealots of Pallas run not in the streets of Amathus.

No. Formerly thou didst watch over the leafy hair of the trees, over the wet flowers, over the heavy and savory fruits. It is for that we chose thee.

Guard thou today our blond heads, the opened poppies of our lips and the violets of our eyes. Guard the firm fruit of our breasts and give us lovers who resemble thee.

CXIV
THE DANCING-GIRL WITH KROTALES

T H O U attachest to thy light hands the resounding krotales, Myr-rhinidion my dear, and, stepping naked from thy robe, thou extendest thy nervous limbs. How pretty thou art, thine arms in the air, thy loins arched and thy breasts reddened!

Thou beginnest: thy feet, one before the other, pose, hesitate, and glide softly. Thy body bends like a scarf, thou caressest thy shivering skin and voluptuousness inundates thy long, swooning eyes.

Suddenly thou strikest the krotales! Arch thyself, erect upon thy feet, shake thy loins, throw out thy legs, and let thy clamoring hands call all the desires in a band about thy turning body.

We, we applaud with great cries, whether, smiling over thy shoulder, thou agitatest with a shiver thy convulsed, muscular croup, or whether thou undulatest, almost extended, to the rhythm of thy memories.

CXV
THE FLUTE PLAYER

M E L I X O , thy legs joined, thy body inclined, thine arms forward, thou slippest thy light, double-flute between thy lips moist with wine and thou playest about the couch where Teleas still embraces me.

Am I not most imprudent, I who hire so young a girl to distract my hours of labor? Am I not thoughtless, I who show her thus naked to the curious looks of my lovers?

No, Melixo, little musician, thou art an honest friend. Yesterday thou didst not refuse to change thy flute for another, when I despaired of accomplishing a love full of difficulties. But thou art safe.

For I know well of what thou thinkest. Thou awaitest the end of this night of excesses which animates thee cruelly and in vain, and, at the first dawn, thou wilt run in the street, with thine only friend Psyllos, to thy little broken mattress.

CXVI
THE WARM GIRDLE

" T H O U thinkest thou lovest me no longer, Teleas, and for a month thou hast passed thy nights at the table, as though the fruits, the wines, the honey, could make thee forget my mouth. Thou thinkest thou lovest me no longer, poor fool!"

Speaking thus, I loosened my moist girdle and I rolled it about his head. It was still quite warm with the heat of my belly; the perfume of my skin issued from its fine meshes.

He breathed it deeply, his eyes closed; then I felt that he returned to me and I even saw very clearly his reawakening desires which he hid not from me; but, as a ruse, I resisted.

"No, my friend! This evening, Lysippos possesses me. Farewell!" And I added, as I fled: "O gormand of fruits and vegetables! the little garden of Bilitis has only one fig, but it is good."

CXVII
TO A HAPPY HUSBAND

I e n v y thee, Agorakrites, for having a wife so zealous. It is she herself who attends to the stable; and in the morning, in place of making love, she gives drink to the cattle.

Thou shouldst rejoice in her. How many others, thou sayest, dream only of base pleasures, awake at night, asleep in the daytime, and yet demanding from adultery a criminal satiety?

Yes; thy wife labors in the stable. They say even that she has a thousand tendernesses for the youngest of thine asses. Ah! Ha! He is a good animal. He has a black spot over his eyes.

They say that she plays between his hooves, under his soft, gray belly. . . . But those who say that are slanderers. If thine ass pleases her, Agorakrites, it is without doubt because she recalls thy look in his.

CXVIII
TO AN ESTRAY

T h e love of women is the most beautiful of all that mortals know; and thou wouldst think so, Kleo, if thou hadst a truly voluptuous soul. But thou dreamest only vanities.

Thou triflest away thy nights in cherishing youths who are ungrateful to us. Look at them! How ugly they are! Compare to their round heads, our thick hair; seek our white breasts upon their chests.

Beside their narrow flanks, consider our luxuriant hips, a broad couch hollowed for a lover. Say, above all, what human lips, save hers they would desire, can perfect the pleasures?

Thou art sick, O Kleo, but a woman can cure thee. Go to young

Satyra, the daughter of my neighbor Gorgo. Her croup is a rose of the sun, and she will not refuse thee the pleasure she herself prefers.

CXIX
INTIMACIES

Thou askest, O Bilitis, why I have become Lesbian? But what player of the flute is not, a little? I am poor; I have no bed; I lie with her who wishes me and I thank her with what I have.

While yet small, we dance naked; those dances: thou knowest them, my dear: the twelve desires of Aphrodite. We regard each other, we compare our nudities and we find them so pretty.

During the long night, we inflame ourselves for the pleasure of the spectators; but our ardor is not feigned and we feel it so much that sometimes, behind the doors, one of us may entice her companion who consents.

How then can we love man, who is rough with us? He takes us as women and leaves us before the delight. Thou, thou art a woman; thou knowest how I feel. Thou canst take it as for thyself.

CXX
THE COMMAND

"Old woman, hear me. I give a festival in three days. It is to divert me. Thou shalt lend me all thy girls. How many hast thou, and what can they do?"

"I have seven. Three dance the kordax with the scarf and the phallos. Nephelis of the sleek armpits will mimic the love of doves between her rosy breasts.

One singer, in a broidered peplos, will chant the songs of Rhodes, accompanied by two auletrides who will have garlands of myrtle rolled about their brown legs."

"It is well. See that they are freshly depilated, bathed, and perfumed from head to foot, ready for other games, if they are demanded. Go give the orders. Farewell."

CXXI
THE FIGURE OF PASIPHÆ

In a debauch that two young men and some courtesans made at my house, where love gushed out like wine, Damalis, in honor of her name, danced the figure of Pasiphæ.

She had caused to be made at Kition two masks of a cow and of a bull, for herself and for Karmantidea. She wore terrible horns, and a hairy tail upon her croup.

The other women, whom I led, holding flowers and torches, circled about with cries, caressing Damalis with the tips of our pendent tresses.

Their lowings and our songs and the dancing of our loins lasted longer than the night. The empty chamber is still warm. I regard my reddened knees and the kanthares of Kios in which are roses floating.

CXXII
THE JUGGLER [24]

WHEN the first dawn blended with the feeble glimmer of the torches, I sent into the orgy a flute-player, vicious and agile, who trembled a little, being cold.

Praise the little girl with blue lids, short hair, pointed breasts, clad only in a girdle from which hung yellow ribbons and the stems of black iris.

Praise her! For she was adroit and performed difficult tricks. She juggled with hoops, without breaking anything in the room; she glided through them like a grasshopper.

Sometimes she made a wheel, bending upon her hands and feet. Or, with her two legs in the air and her knees apart, she curved herself backward and touched the ground, laughing.

CXXIII
THE DANCE OF THE FLOWERS

ANTHIS, dancing girl from Lydia, has seven veils about her. She unrolls the yellow veil; her black hair spreads out. The rosy veil slips from her mouth. The white veil falls, revealing her naked arms.

She releases her little breasts from the red veil which loosens itself. She lets fall the green veil from her double, rounded croup. She draws the blue veil from her shoulders, but she presses upon her puberty the last transparent veil.

The young men supplicate her; she tosses her head backward. Only at the sound of the flutes, she tears it a little; then, suddenly, and with the gestures of the dance, she culls the flowers of her body.

Singing: "Where are my roses? Where are my perfumed violets? Where are my tufts of parsley?—Behold my roses; I give them to you. Behold my violets; will you have them? Behold my pretty, curling parsley." [25]

CXXIV
VIOLENCE

No, thou shalt not take me by force; count not on that, Lamprias. If thou hast heard it said that someone violated Parthenis, know that she abetted it; for no one plays with us without being invited.

Oh! do thy best; make efforts. See: it is a failure. I scarcely defend myself, yet. I will not call for help. And I do not even struggle; but I dodge. Poor friend, it is a failure again.

Continue. This little game amuses me. The more so as I am sure to conquer. Again an unhappy essay and perhaps thou wilt be less disposed to show me thine extinguished desires.

Butcher, what doest thou! Cur! thou art breaking my wrists! And this knee, this knee which forces me open! Ah! Go now. It is a fine victory, that of ravishing a young girl, in tears, upon the ground.

CXXV
SONG

The first gave me a collar, a collar of pearls, worth a city with its palaces and temples, its treasures and its slaves.

The second made verses for me. He said that my tresses were black as those of the night and my eyes blue as those of the morning.

The third was so beautiful that his mother could not embrace him without blushing. He placed his hands upon my knees and his lips upon my naked foot.

Thou, thou hast told me nothing, thou hast given me nothing, for thou art poor. And thou art not beautiful, but it is thee I love.

CXXVI
ADVICE TO A LOVER

If thou wouldst be loved by a woman, O young friend, whoever she may be, tell her not that thou wishest her, but let her see thee every day; then disappear, to return.

If she address her speech to thee, be amorous without eagerness. She, of herself, will come to thee. But thou must take her by force, the day when she intends to give herself.

When thou receivest her in thy bed, neglect thine own pleasure. The hands of an amorous woman are trembling and without caresses. Excuse them from being zealous.

But thou, take no repose. Prolong thy kisses to breathlessness. Allow her no sleep, even though she beg it of thee. Kiss always that part of her body toward which she turns her eyes.

CXXVII
FRIENDS AT DINNER

MYROMERIS and Maskale, my friends, come with me, for I have no lover this evening and, lying upon beds of byssos, we will converse over our dinner.

A night of repose will do you good; you shall sleep in my bed, even without fards and with undressed hair. Wear a simple tunic of wool and leave your jewels in their box.

No one shall make you dance to admire your legs and the heavy movements of your loins. No one shall demand the Sacred Figures to judge whether you are amorous.

And I have not commanded for us two flute-players with pretty mouths, but two pots of browned peas, cakes of honey, fried croquettes, and my last leathern bottle of Kios.

CXXVIII
THE TOMB OF A YOUNG COURTESAN

HERE lies the delicate body of Lydé, little dove, the most joyous of all the courtesans, who, more than all others, loved orgies and floating hair, soft dances and tunics of hyacinth.

More than all others, she loved the pleasant mingling of tongues, caresses upon her cheek, games that only the lamp saw, and the love which bruises the limbs. And now she is a little shadow.

But, before putting her in the tomb, they arranged her hair marvelously and laid her in roses; even the stone which covers her is all impregnated with essences and perfumes.

Sacred earth, nurse of all, receive gently the poor dead. Let her sleep in thine arms, O Mother, and may there grow about her stele, not nettles and briers, but tender white violets.

CXXIX
THE LITTLE ROSE MERCHANT [26]

"Yesterday," Nais said to me, "I was in the market when a little girl in red tatters, carrying roses, passed before a group of young men. And this is what I heard:

'Buy something from me.—Explain thyself, little one, for we know not what thou sellest. Thyself? Thy roses? Or all together? —If you will buy from me all these flowers, you may have mine for nothing.

'And how much wishest thou for thy roses?—I must have six oboli for my mother, else I shall be beaten like a bitch.—Follow us. Thou shalt have a drachma.—Then shall I go for my little sister?'

"And both followed those men. They had no breasts, Bilitis. They knew not even how to smile. They trotted along like kids which one leads to the butcher."

CXXX
THE DISPUTE

Ah! By Aphrodite, behold thee! outrage! rottenness! infection! sterile one! carcanet! clumsy! good-for-nothing! evil sow! Do not try to escape me; come yet nearer.

Behold this woman of the sailors, who knows not even how to fold her garment on the shoulder, and who uses fard so badly that the black of her brows runs over her cheek in floods of ink!

Thou art Phœnician; lie with those of thy race. As for me, my father was Hellene: I have right over all those who wear the petasos. And even over the others, if it pleases me so.

Pause not in my street again, or I will send thee to Hades to make love to Karon and I will say very justly: "Let the earth cover thee lightly!" [27]—so that the dogs may dig thee out.

CXXXI
MELANCHOLY

I shiver; the night is cool, and all the forest wet. Why hast thou led me here? Is not my wide bed softer than this moss strewn with stones?

My flowery robe will be spotted with verdure; my hair will be tangled with twigs; my neck: look at my neck: already it is soiled by the damp earth.

Formerly, I followed into the woods he who... Ah! Leave me for a while. I am sad, this evening. Leave me, without speaking, my hand over my eyes.

In truth, canst thou not wait! Are we beasts, to take each other so! Leave me. Thou shalt open neither my knees nor my lips. Even my eyes shall stay closed, lest they weep.

CXXXII

THE LITTLE PHANION

STRANGER, pause; see who is signing to thee: it is little Phanion of Kôs. She merits that thou shouldst choose her.

See, her hair is curled like parsley, her skin is smooth as the down of a bird. She is small and brown. She speaks nicely.

If thou wouldst follow her, she would not demand of thee all the money from thy voyage; no, only a drachma or a pair of slippers.

Thou wilt find, at her house, a good bed,[28] fresh figs, milk, wine; and, if it be cold, there will be a fire.

CXXXIII

INDICATIONS

PASSER-BY who pauses, if thou wishest slender thighs and nervous loins, a firm throat, knees that clasp, go to Plango; she is my friend.

If thou seekest a laughing girl with exuberant breasts, delicately shaped, the croup plump and the loins hollowed, go to the corner of this street, where Spidhorodellis dwells.

But if long tranquil hours in the arms of a courtesan, a soft skin, a warm body and fragrant hair please thee, seek Milto and thou wilt be content.

Expect not much love, but avail thyself of its experience. One may demand all from a woman when she is naked, when it is night, and when the hundred drachmæ are upon the hearth.

CXXXIV

THE MERCHANT OF WOMEN

"WHO is there?—I am the merchant of women. Open the door, Sostrata; I offer thee two opportunities. This is the first. Approach, Anasyrtolis, and strip thyself.—She is a trifle large."

"She is a beauty. Beside, she dances the kordax and she knows eighty songs.—Turn thyself. Raise thine arms. Display thy hair. Give me thy foot. Smile. It is well."

"Now this one.—She is too young!—Not at all; she was twelve years old the day before yesterday, and thou wilt teach her nothing. —Remove thy tunic. Let me see. No; she is thin."

"I ask but one mina.—And the first?—Two minæ, thirty.— Three minæ for the two?—It is said.—Enter there and bathe your-selves. And thou, farewell."

CXXXV
THE STRANGER

Stranger, go not farther into the city. Thou wilt not find else-where girls younger or more expert than mine. I am Sostrata, re-nowned beyond the sea.

See this one whose eyes are green as water in the grass. Thou wouldst not have her? Here are other eyes which are black as violets, and hair three cubits long.

I have better still. Xantho, open thy cyclas. Stranger, these breasts are hard as quinces; touch them. And her pretty belly, thou seest, carries the three folds of Kypris.

I bought her with her sister, who is not yet of the age for love but who will second her usefully. By the two goddesses! Thou art of a noble race. Phyllis and Xantho, follow the illustrious one!

CXXXVI
THE REMEMBRANCE OF MNASIDIKA

They danced, one before the other, with rapid, flying movements; they seemed always wishing to embrace and yet did not even touch, unless with the tips of their lips.

When they turned their backs in dancing, they looked at each other, the head upon the shoulder, the perspiration gleaming under their lifted arms, and their delicate hair gliding across their breasts.

The languor of their eyes, the fire of their cheeks, the gravity of their faces, were three ardent songs. They grazed each other furtively; they bent their bodies upon their hips.

And suddenly they fell, to finish the soft dance upon the ground. ... Remembrance of Mnasidika, it was then thou camest to me; and all, except thy dear image, troubled me.

CXXXVII
THE YOUNG MOTHER

BELIEVE not, Myromeris, that, in becoming a mother, thou hast lessened thy beauty. See how thy body, beneath thy robe, has drowned its slim form in a voluptuous softness.

Thy breasts are two vast flowers, reversed upon thy chest, whose cut stems give out a milky sap. Thy softened belly swoons beneath the hand.

And, beside, consider the tiny babe, born of a quiver which thou didst feel one evening, in the arms of a passer-by whose name thou dost not even know. Dream of her distant destiny.

Her eyes, which now scarcely open, will some day be elongated in a line of black fard, and they will sow among men sorrow or joy by one movement of their lashes.

CXXXVIII
THE UNKNOWN

HE sleeps. I know him not. He horrifies me. Nevertheless, his purse is filled with gold and he gave four drachmæ to the slave on entering. I expect a mina for myself.

But I told the Phrygian to enter the bed in my place. He was drunk and took her for me. I would rather die in torment than stretch myself out near this man.

Alas! I dream of the meadows of Tauros.... I was a little virgin.... Then I had a light heart and I was so mad with amorous envy that I hated my married sisters.

What would I not have done to obtain that which I refused this night! Today, my breasts are drooping and, in my exhausted heart, Eros slumbers from lassitude.

CXXXIX
THE CHEAT

I AWAKEN.... Is he then gone! He has left something? No: two empty amphoras and some soiled flowers. All the rug is red with wine.

I have slept, but I am still drunk.... With whom, then, did I return? ... At least, we lay down together. Even the bed is drenched with sweat.

Perhaps there were several; the bed is so disordered. I know not.... But someone saw them! There is my Phrygian. She still sleeps across the door.

I kick her in the breast, and I cry: "Bitch, thou couldst not..." I am so hoarse that I can say no more.

CXL
THE LAST LOVER

CHILD, do not pass without loving me. I am still beautiful in the night; thou shalt see how much warmer my autumn[29] is than the springtime of another.

Seek not for love from virgins. Love is a difficult art in which young girls are little versed. I have prepared it all my life to give it to my last lover.

Thou shalt be my last lover; I know it. Behold my mouth, for which a nation has paled with desire. Behold my hair, the same hair which Psappha the Great has sung.

I will gather for thee all that remains of my lost youth. I will burn even the memories. I will give thee the flute of Lykas, the girdle of Mnasidika.

CXLI
THE DOVE

FOR a long time I have been beautiful; the day comes when I shall no longer be a woman. And then I shall know heart-rending memories, burning, solitary envy, and tears in my hands.

If life is a long dream, of what good to resist? Now, four and five times a night, I demand amorous enjoyment; and when my loins are exhausted, I sink asleep wherever my body falls.

In the morning, I open my eyelids and I shiver in my hair. A dove is at my window; I ask of her in what month we are. She says to me: "It is the month when women are in love."

Ah! Whatever be the month, the dove speaks truly, Kypris. And I throw my two arms about my lover and, with great tremblings, I stretch my still benumbed legs to the foot of the bed.

CXLII
THE RAIN OF MORNING

T H E night has passed. The stars are far away. See, the last courtesans have returned with their lovers. And I, in the rain of morning, I write these verses on the sand.

The leaves are laden with brilliant water. The rivulets across the paths drag along the earth and the dead leaves. The rain, drop by drop, makes holes in my song.

Oh! How sad and alone I am here! The young regard me not; the old have forgotten me. It is well. They will learn my verses, they and the children of their children.

That is what neither Myrtale nor Thaïs nor Glykera may say, the day when their lovely cheeks shall be wrinkled. Those who will love after me will sing my strophes together.

CXLIII
THE TRUE DEATH [30]

A P H R O D I T E, merciless goddess, thou hast willed that, for me also, the happy youth of beautiful hair shall vanish in a few days. Why am I less than dead!

I regard myself in my mirror; I have no longer smiles nor tears. O sweet face which loved Mnasidika, I cannot believe that thou wert mine.

Can it be that all is ended? I have not yet lived five times eight years; it seems to me that I was born only yesterday; and now, behold, I must say: No one will love me more.

All my cut hair I have twisted into my girdle, and I offer it to thee, Kypris Eternal! I will never cease to adore thee. This is the last verse of the pious Bilitis.

IV
THE TOMB OF BILITIS

THE TOMB OF BILITIS

⋙ ⋘

FIRST EPITAPH

IN the country where the springs are born from the sea and where the river beds are shelving rocks, I, Bilitis, was born.

My mother was Phœnician; my father, Damophylos, Hellene. My mother taught me the songs of Byblos, sad as the first dawn.

I have adored Astarte at Kypros. I have known Psappha at Lesbos. I have sung as I have loved. If I have lived well, Passer-by, tell it to thy daughter.

And sacrifice not for me a black goat; but, in soft libation, press her teats above my tomb.

SECOND EPITAPH

UPON the sombre banks of Melas, at Tamassos in Pamphylia, I, Bilitis, daughter of Damophylos, was born. Thou seest, I rest far from my native land.

As a child, I learned the loves of Adonis and of Astarte, the mysteries of the holy Seris, and the death and return to Her-Of-The-Rounded-Eyes.

If I have been a courtesan, what is the harm? Was it not my duty as a woman? Stranger, the Mother-Of-All-Things guides us. To disregard her is not prudent.

In gratitude to thee who has paused, I wish thee this destiny: Mayest thou be loved, but never love. Farewell; remember thou, in thine old age, that thou hast seen my tomb.

LAST EPITAPH

UNDER the black leaves of the laurels, under the amorous blooms of the roses, it is here that I lie, I who have woven line with line, embellishing the kiss.

I grew up in the land of the nymphs; I lived on the isle of

lovers; I died on the isle of Kypros. It is for this that my name is illustrious and my stele polished with oil.

Weep not for me, thou who pausest; my funeral rites were beautiful; the weepers tore their cheeks. They have laid in my tomb my mirrors and my necklaces.

And now, over the pale meadows of asphodel, I walk, an impalpable shadow; and the remembrance of my earthly life is the joy of my life in the underworld.

V
BIBLIOGRAPHY
AND NOTES

BIBLIOGRAPHY

꙳≫ ≪꙳

I. THE SONGS OF BILITIS, issued [in German] for the first time; with a Glossary, by G. Heim.—Leipzig, 1894.

II. THE SONGS OF BILITIS, translated from the Greek [into French] for the first time, by P. L.—Paris, 1895.

III. SIX SONGS OF BILITIS, translated into verse [in French], by Madame Jean Bertheroy.—*Revue pour les Jeunes Filles*. Paris, Armand Colin, 1896.

IV. TWENTY-SIX SONGS OF BILITIS, translated [into German] by Richard Dehmel.—*Die Gesellschaft*, Leipzig, 1896.

V. TWENTY SONGS OF BILITIS, translated [into German] by Dr. Paul Goldmann.—*Frankfurter Zeitung*, 1896.

VI. THE SONGS OF BILITIS [in German], by Prof. von Willamovitz-Moellendorf.—*Gœttingsche Gelehrte*.—Gœttingue, 1896.

VII. EIGHT SONGS OF BILITIS, translated [into Czech] by Alexandre Backovsky.—Prague, 1897.

III. FOUR SONGS OF BILITIS, translated [into Swedish] by Gustav Uddgren. —*Nordisk Revy*.—Stockholm, 1897.

IX. THREE SONGS OF BILITIS [in French], set to music by Claude Debussy.—Paris, Fromont, 1898.

NOTES

TO THE SONGS OF BILITIS

—»» ««—

1. Psappha.—"As she spelled her name in her soft Æolic dialect."
(Robinson.)

On the testimony of common-sense, and of many writers of antiquity, who, at least, had more on which to base an opinion than we have, Pierre Louÿs' description in *Song* xlvi ("Psappha") of ". . . her hair is cut like that of an athlete . . . virile breast . . . narrow hips . . ." and, as assumed, ready to prey lasciviously upon any passer-by, seems absurd and defamatory. Sappho's brother, Larichus, was public cup-bearer at Mytilene, an office held only by young men of noble birth. She herself, "violet-weaving, pure, soft-smiling" as Alcæus says, although "small and dark" according to Maximus Tyrius, was, according to her own words, "of a quiet temper" and, in all probability, was married and the mother of a daughter named Cleis whom she mentions in an extant fragment (Wharton, 72), which, considering the personal tone of so many of her poems, may be taken as something more than a poetic fancy. "I have a fair daughter with a form like a golden flower, Cleis the beloved, above whom I prize nor all Lydia nor lovely Lesbos." Philoxenos describes her as "sweet-voiced." Damokaris, in the *Anthology* (Plan. App. xvi, 310) describes her picture in glowing terms: "Her eyes overflow with brilliance, showing a fancy rich in happy images. Her skin, smooth and not too reddened, shows simplicity; and the blended gaiety and gravity of her features proclaims the union, in her, of the Muse and Kypris."

That she gathered about her a society of maidens to whom she taught the Art of Poetry is well known; the names of many of her pupils and friends have been preserved in fragments of her verse. How much further her friendships were carried, as suggested in some of her poems, will always be a matter of speculation; but that she was a charming, lovely woman, sufficiently reserved, of perfect maturity and free from petty or promiscuous vice, seems undeniable, otherwise, we may be sure the writers of antiquity would have treated her with far less admiration and respect than they did.

2. This verse of Sappho's is placed by Pierre Louÿs on the half-title of the section in his book entitled "Elegiacs at Mytilene."

3. The crime of which Phryne was accused, and for which she was tried before the Areopagos at Athens, was that of profaning the Eleusinian

Mysteries—a crime even more serious than Pierre Louÿs' "Murder."

4. This quotation from Theocritos translated reads: "Sweet too is my music, whether I make melody on pipe, or discourse on the flute, or reed, or flageolet." (xx. 28-29. LANG.)

5. *Song* xii.—French, *Bergeronnette*; Latin, *Passer*. A species of sparrow, but not necessarily our "English sparrow." Various living things were sacred to Aphrodite, as symbolic of her diverse attributes. The sparrow symbolized productivity.

6. *Song* xiv.—That is "bee." Marcus Argentarius has an epigram in the *Anthology* using the word: "Melissa is thy name and truly so, as my heart bears witness. Thy soft lips sweeten thy kisses with honey, but thou also piercest with a cruel sting." (Anth. Pal. v. 32).

7. *Song* xvi.—The "amphora kiss," as though one drank the kiss from a beaker with two handles.

8. *Song* xlii.—Execrations of the morning light were popular among the Greek amatory poets. See, among others, Meleager: "Star of Morning, enemy of lovers, why shinest thou so quickly upon the couch where, a moment since, I lay warm with Demo? . . ." (Anth. Pal. v. 172).

9. *Song* xliii.—The same thought is in the "Song of Songs" (Song of Solomon, i, 17): "The beams of our house are of cedar and our rafters of fir."

10. This quotation from Sappho (referred to above in *Note 2*), translated reads: "Mnasidika is more shapely than the tender Gyrinno." (WHARTON, 76.)

11. *Song* xlvi.—John Addington Symonds, in his *Problem in Greek Ethics* (London, 1901, pp. 71-72), remarks: "Lesbian passion, as the Greeks called it, never obtained the same social sanction as boy-love. It is significant that Greek Mythology offers no legends of the goddesses parallel to those which consecrated pæderastia among the male deities. Again, we have no recorded example, so far as I can remember, of noble friendships between women rising into political and historical prominence. . . . The Greeks, while tolerating, regarded it rather as an eccentricity of nature, or a vice, than as an honourable and socially useful emotion. . . . There is an important passage in the *Amores* of Lucian which proves that the Greeks felt an abhorrence of sexual inversion among women similar to that which moderns· feel for its manifestation among men. . . . And . . . while the love of males for males in Greece obtained moralization and reached the high position of a recognized social function, the love of female for female remained undeveloped and unhonoured, on the same level as both forms of homosexual passion in the modern European world are."

 The exposition, perhaps beyond decorum, of Lesbian love in this section of the *Songs of Bilitis* has no parallel in all Greek literature, where references to the subject are very few.

12. *Song* liii.—In *Aphrodite* (1, 7), Pierre Louÿs has given a description

of this custom as carried out at Ephesos. I have been unable to locate any classic authority for the description.

13. *Song* LVIII.—"The pleasant cave and shadowy, sacred to the nymphs that are called the Naiads." (Odyssey, XIII. LANG). In "the secret places of this wondrous cave," at Athene's suggestion, Odysseos hides his treasure, and there he is transformed into an old man, as a disguise to conceal him from Penelope's wooers.

14. *Song* LXXI.—See *Sappho* (WHARTON, 2): ". . . For when I see thee but a little, I have no utterance left, my tongue is broken down, and straightway a subtle fire has run under my skin. With my eyes I have no sight, my ears ring, sweat pours down, and a trembling seizes all my body; I am paler than grass, and seem in my madness little better than one dead. . . ."

15. *Song* LXXV.—See the sixth mime of *Herondas*. This mime describes a visit between two women in reference to the same sort of object enquired for by Bilitis' friend. One of Herondas' ladies remarks, about the leather-worker: "He works at his house and sells secretly.—Every door is afraid of the tax-collectors!—But the things he makes, all of them, are worthy of Athena. . . . Hunt as you might, you could not find another cobbler so kindly disposed toward women." (BUCK.)

16. *Song* LXXXI.—See Meleager: "Truly, thou betrayest thyself; thy locks, still moist with perfumes, denounce thy dissolute life; thine eyes, heavy with fatigue, show well how thy night has been passed; this coronal upon thy forehead reveals the festival; this disordered hair shows the path of amorous hands; and all thy body staggers under the vapors of the wine. . . ." (Anth. Pal. v. 175.)

17. *Song* LXXXIII.—See Paulus Silentiarius: "For whom curl my hair? for whom trim my nails? for whom perfume my hands? To what end this purple-banded cloak, since I go not to beautiful Rhodopis? . . ." (Anth. Pal. v. 228.)

18. This quotation from Philodemos translated reads: "Bind my head with narcissus and let me taste the crooked flute. Anoint my limbs with saffron ointment, wet my gullet with wine of Mytilene and mate me with a virgin who will love her nest." (Anth. Pal. XI, 34, PATON).

19. *Song* XCIV.—The thyrsos as carried by votaries of Dionysos was usually a long rod with a pine cone fastened upright on the end. Sometimes a tall umbellifer (Narthex) was used, stripped of its leaves up to the top, leaving only the umbellar blossoms. In either case they were too long to be used as drum-sticks.

20. *Song* CI.—See Philodemos: "I salute thee.—I salute thee also.—What is thy name?—And thine? Thou mayest know mine later.—Thou art in a hurry?—And thou art not?—Hast thou someone?—I have always my lover.—Wilt thou eat dinner with me today?—If thou wishest.—Good. What shall I give thee?—Give me nothing in advance.—That is strange.—But when the night is over, give what thou wishest.—Thou art a just girl. Where is thy dwelling? I will send for thee.—I will

show thee.—And when wilt thou come?—At once, if thou wishest.—
At once, then.—Lead the way." (Anth. Pal. v. 46.)

21. *Song* cɪɪɪ.—See Asclepiades: "Upon a day, I played with facile Her-
mione. Like the Goddess, she wore a girdle broidered with flowers;
and on it I read, in letters of gold: 'Love me, but grieve not if I give
myself to another.' " (Anth. Pal. v. 158.)

22. *Song* cɪv.—In the original, "un batelier du port," literally, "a boatman of the port," which translates simply as "boatman." The most
extensive cogitations have failed to clear up this obscure passage. Possibly
Pierre Louÿs intended to convey the thought that the ecstasy transfigured a common boatman into a "divine image." But the nearest approach to a solution (and the one which the artist has chosen to illus-
trate), is that suggested in Secundus (xɪɪɪ), according to the eighteenth
century translation:

> *"With am'rous Strife exanimate I lay,*
> *   Around your Neck my languid Arm I threw;*
> *My trembling Heart had just forgot to play,*
> *   Its vital Spirit from my Bosom flew:*
> *The Stygian Lake; the dreary Realms below,*
> *   To which the Sun a cheering Beam denies;*
> *Old Charon's Boat, slow-wand'ring to and fro,*
> *   Promiscuous pass'd before my swimming Eyes."*
> *   Etc., etc.*

23. *Song* cɪx.—Artemis was more likely to be seen bathing with disastrous
results to the spectator, as noted in the legend of Actæon.

24. *Song* cxxɪɪ.—A much better piece of work than Automedon's epigram
on a similar subject (Anth. Pal. v. 129).

25. *Song* cxxɪɪɪ.—This Song is quoted by Athenæus (Deipnosophists, xɪv,
27).

26. *Song* cxxɪx.—See Dionysos: "Little vendor of roses, thou art as fair as
thine own flowers. But what sellest thou? thyself? or thy roses? or both
together?" (Anth. Pal. v. 81.)

27. *Song* cxxx.—The hope, frequently expressed in the *Sepulchral Epi-*
grams. See Meleager: "Hail, Earth, Mother of all! To him who bore
so lightly upon thee, Aesigenes, mayest thou now be equally light."
(Anth. Pal. vɪɪ. 461. Englished from Pierre Louÿs' translation.) The
less flattering interpretation of the hope is expressed by Ammianus:
"May the dust be light on thee when under earth, wretched Nearchus,
so that the dogs may easily dig thee out." (Anth. Pal. xɪ. 226. PATON.)

28. *Song* cxxxɪɪ.—See Antipater: "For a drachma one may have Europa the
Athenian, without fear of rivals or refusals. She has a soft bed and,
if the night is cold, a fire. Surely, O Zeus, there was no need for thee
to make thyself a bull!" (Anth. Pal. v. 109.) See also Philodemos:
"Philenion is small and brown, but her hair is curled like parsley and
her skin is soft as down. . . ." (Anth. Pal. v. 121.)

29. *Song* CXL.—See Paulus Silentiarius: "Philinna, thy wrinkles are preferable to the fresh tints of young girls. I love less in my hands their straight, hard breasts, than thine which incline like full-blown roses. Thine autumn is fairer than their springtime; their summer is colder than thy time of snows." (Anth. Pal. v. 258.)

30. *Song* CXLIII.—Compare Rufinus: "Once I had soft skin, firm breasts and pretty feet; my body was supple, mine eyebrows arched, my hair undulating. Time has changed all. Not one treasure of my youth remains; . . ." (Anth. Pal. v. 76.)

    For the theme developed, see François Villon's "Les regrets de la belle Heaulmière."

C A P R I C O R N   T I T L E S

201. *Hauser,* DIET DOES IT. $1.35.
202. *Moscati,* ANCIENT SEMITIC CIVILIZATIONS. $1.65.
203. CHIN P'ING MEI. $2.95.
204. *Brockelman,* HISTORY OF ISLAMIC PEOPLES. $2.45.
205. *Salter,* CONDITIONED REFLEX THERAPY. $1.85.
206. *Lissner,* LIVING PAST. $2.45.
207. *Davis,* CORPORATIONS. $2.45.
208. *Rodman,* CONVERSATIONS WITH ARTISTS. $1.65.
209. *Falls,* GREAT WAR. $1.95.
210. MEMOIRS OF A RENAISSANCE POPE. $1.95.
211. *Schachner,* FOUNDING FATHERS. $2.45.
212. *Viereck,* UNADJUSTED MAN. $1.85.
213. *Cournos,* TREASURY OF CLASSIC RUSSIAN LITERATURE. $2.45.
215. *Guerdan,* BYZANTIUM. $1.45.
216. *Mandeville,* FABLE OF THE BEES. $1.65.
217. *Bradford,* OF PLYMOUTH PLANTATION. $1.65.
218. *Taylor,* COURSE OF GERMAN HISTORY. $1.65.
219. *Frankfurter,* LAW & POLITICS. $1.75.
220. *Shelby Little,* GEORGE WASHINGTON. $1.95.
221. *Peterson,* ANCIENT MEXICO. $1.95.
223. *Isaacs,* IMAGES OF ASIA. $1.85.
224 *Krafft Ebing,* ABERRATIONS OF SEXUAL LIFE. $1.95.
226. *Grekov,* SOVIET CHESS. $1.65.
227. *Ernst-Loth,* REPORT ON THE AMERICAN COMMUNIST. $1.45.
228. *Adler,* THE PROBLEM CHILD. $1.85.
231. *Fine,* FIFTY CHESS LESSONS. $1.45.
233. *Barraclough,* ORIGINS OF MODERN GERMANY. $2.45.
235. *Skeat,* ETYMOLOGICAL DICTIONARY. $2.45.
236. *Hauser,* GAYLORD HAUSER COOK BOOK. $1.45.
237. *Fulop Miller,* THE JESUITS. $2.45.
238. *Shenton,* RECONSTRUCTION. $1.75.
239. *Blitzer,* COMMONWEALTH OF ENGLAND. $1.65.
240. *Wright,* GREAT AMERICAN GENTLEMAN. $1.65.
241. *Braeman,* ROAD TO INDEPENDENCE. $1.65.
242. *Bridenbaugh,* CITIES IN THE WILDERNESS. $2.65.
243. *Bridenbaugh,* CITIES IN REVOLT. $2.65.
244. *de Riencourt,* COMING CAESARS. $1.95.
246. *Weinberg,* THE MUCKRAKERS. $2.45.
247. *Hays,* FROM APE TO ANGEL. $2.65.
248. *James,* ANCIENT GODS. $2.25.
249. *Green,* LUTHER AND THE REFORMATION. $1.65.
250. *Filler,* THE ANXIOUS YEARS. $1.95.
251. *Ehrlich,* EHRLICH'S BLACKSTONE: RIGHTS OF PERSONS, RIGHTS OF THINGS. $2.95.
252. *Ehrlich,* EHRLICH'S BLACKSTONE: PRIVATE WRONGS, PUBLIC WRONGS. $2.95.
253. *Lissner,* THE CAESARS. $1.95.